The Queen of Peace Room

Life Writing Series

In the **Life Writing Series**, Wilfrid Laurier University Press publishes life writing and new life-writing criticism in order to promote autobiographical accounts, diaries, letters, and testimonials written and/or told by women and men whose political, literary, or philosophical purposes are central to their lives. **Life Writing** features the accounts of ordinary people, written in English, or translated into English from French or the languages of the First Nations or from any of the languages of immigration to Canada. **Life Writing** will also publish original theoretical investigations about life writing, as long as they are not limited to one author or text.

Priority is given to manuscripts that provide access to those voices that have not traditionally had access to the publication process.

Manuscripts of social, cultural, and historical interest that are considered for the series, but are not published, are maintained in the **Life Writing Archive** of Wilfrid Laurier University Library.

Series Editor
Marlene Kadar
Humanities Division, York University

Manuscripts to be sent to
Brian Henderson, Director
Wilfrid Laurier University Press
75 University Avenue West
Waterloo, Ontario, Canada N2L 3C5

The Queen of Peace Room

Magie Dominic

Wilfrid Laurier University Press

We acknowledge the support of the Canada Council for the Arts for our publishing program. We acknowledge the financial support of the Government of Canada through the Book Publishing Industry Development Program for our publishing activities.

National Library of Canada Cataloguing in Publication Data

Dominic, Magie, 1944-
   The Queen of Peace room / Magie Dominic.

(Life writing series)
Includes bibliographical references.
ISBN 0-88920-417-9

   1. Dominic, Magie, 1944- .   2. Adult child sexual abuse victims—
Biography.   3. Abused wives—Biography.   I. Title.   II. Series.

HV6626.D65 2002   362.74'092   C2002-903298-9

© 2002 Wilfrid Laurier University Press
Waterloo, Ontario, Canada N2L 3C5
www.wlupress.wlu.ca

Cover design by Leslie Macredie, using artwork by Magie Dominic
(*Untitled Child*, collage with semi-precious stones, photograph,
telephone book cover, antique lace, and dried flowers).
All drawings by Magie Dominic.

Printed in Canada

For my daughter, Heather Rose

In the immense court of my memory…I come to meet myself.
— Augustine of Hippo

Things come apart easily when they have been held together with lies.
— Dorothy Allison

A change in the state of the psyche produces a change in the structure of the body.
— Aristotle

Nature is like parting a curtain; you go inside it.
— Agnes Martin

CONTENTS

Acknowledgments

I would like to give very special thanks to Brian Henderson, Director of Wilfrid Laurier University Press, for having such faith in me. I thank him for his guidance and encouragement, without which I would never have been able to write this book. Thank you to my editor, Jacqueline Larson, for knowing precisely what I was thinking and for her meticulous attention to detail. Thank you to Leslie Macredie and everyone at Wilfrid Laurier University Press for all their work along the way. I am very grateful.

Thank you to Michael Randazzo and Allan Jones of New School University for letting me disappear behind the computers to type and scan; to the League of Canadian Poets for treasured correspondence; to Lynn Samuels of WABC Radio, for her spirit and unyielding words of encouragement; to Don Forst, editor of *The Village Voice*, for taking an interest in my writing at a pivotal point in my life; to the editorial collective at *CV2* (Contemporary Verse 2); to *Prairie Journal* and *ARC Quarterly*; to Dr. Orrin Devinsky for his conversations and knowledge regarding epilepsy; to a group of gentle nuns I met unexpectedly, who changed my life forever; and finally, thank you to Heather Rose, my daughter, for listening to the very first words.

A small portion of chapter 2 and chapter 3 were published in the form of essays under separate titles in the anthologies, *Pushing the Limits* and *Countering the Myths* (Toronto: Women's Press, 1996).

LITURGY OF THE HOURS

Ancient instructions from Saint Benedict, a wealthy Italian who abandoned everything in the fourteenth century, lived as a hermit, and then
moved into a monastery with a book of instruction he'd written, *A Little
Rule for Beginners*. Now it's called *The Holy Rules*, an unceasing round of
prayer on schedule every few hours within the confines of a monastery
or holy place.

- Matins, 12 A.M. midnight, the great prayer of the night.
- Lauds, 3 A.M., praise for the approaching new day.
- Prime, 6 A.M., asking blessing for the day.
- Terce, 9 A.M., "the third hour" in the ancient world, when the
  Holy Spirit came down upon the apostles.
- Sext, 12 noon, time of the midday meal.
- None, 3 P.M., afternoon reflection.
- Vespers, 6 P.M., evening prayer, a longer and formal prayer of
  beauty.
- Compline, 9 P.M., an intimate and quiet prayer closing the day
  and before the singing of matins.

The calculation of these hours varies depending on how ancient the
tradition is and the names change order but the principle is always
the same.

INTRODUCTION

> Just as a country can be the site of a battle, so too can a body
> be the scene of a crime.

The blood I am walking through is splattered over a black wooden
floor, which makes it impossible to detect until I'm almost stepping in
it. I have to stare and see where the light is bouncing. The light guides
me as it spills from giant bulbs mounted on high poles. The incline of
the slick wooden floor makes everything difficult. It forces me to slow
down, grabbing clothing as I move. A cape lying dangerously close to a
pool of blood, gloves thrown into a corner, fabric tossed onto floor-
boards, a tiny headpiece. I watch as my feet move through rivulets of
blood and grab clothing with both hands, every move calculated with
heart-pounding speed, like choreography. Not a second to waste. Then
exit, same side I entered from, stage left, the Metropolitan Opera,
Saturday afternoon, live, on the air. I leave John the Baptist's blood running down the tilted stage of the Met. I leave Salome with blood dripping down the front of her crème dress. I leave the sounds of thousands of people applauding on the other side of the giant, gold curtain
and hang my dresser bag from a high rack in the wardrobe room. All
the racks at the Met are high. It isn't just that I'm short. The racks are
unusually high to accommodate elaborate costumes. I unplug the iron
and steamer, close the heavy wardrobe room door, leave the images of
violence, and return home to think. To the quiet.

Anything can trigger memories, a voice, a story, a smell, the sight
of dripping blood. And images come roaring back into the mind as

1

from a dam, broken, unstoppable. I walk up the crumbling steps of my building, into the apartment and click on the radio. One announcement: "All the men will die from AIDS and all the women will die from cancer and animals will inhabit the earth again."

I snap the radio off. I don't need to know this. But it's too late. I know it now.

The television screen has enormous red-painted lips on it, huge glossy lips. They almost fill the screen. The TV is saying, "I love you, I love you, watch me, watch me." I recognize manipulation and snap the TV off too. Put a cloth and vase of flowers over the rectangular shape. "Watch me, watch me" I imagine it calling from beneath the cloth. I remove the TV, leave it on the street, and return home again. Maybe now I can think. The electrical outlet beckons, "I wanted you to watch me. I wanted you to watch me."

I leave the apartment and its electrical outlets and travel to an isolated retreat house at the suggestion of a friend. I'm told along the way that there's something unique about the place, something positive, but not explainable.

Traditional Chinese medicine holds that there are as many as 2000 acupuncture points on the human body, which are connected by 20 points (12 main, 8 secondary) called meridians.

— "All About Acupuncture"

Along the major meridians were found particularly sensitive energy points called hsüeh, which function as energy relay terminals, much as transformers along power lines do.

— Daniel Reid, *The Complete Book of Chinese Health and Healing*

FRIDAY, MIDNIGHT

I arrive in a friend's car. Almost everything is pitch-black except for porch lights. Things are lit by stars and a moon. Except there is no moon. Only the dark of the moon, somewhere between July 8th and 9th. The dew-covered ground is slippery under foot. We walk to a large wooden house, ring an ancient doorbell, wake someone I can hear getting up in the middle of the night. A woman opens the door. A second woman stands behind her. I'm introduced to them in the middle of the night, in the middle of the woods. One woman is named Sister Marie, the other Sister Joan. The four of us walk up a small hill, and across the grass to a large brick building. Sister Marie punches a secret code into the locked door, turns her flashlight off, and holds the door open.

There's a large empty bulletin board marked *Messages*, to the right. A sign points towards an unseen pay phone. We walk together down a hallway to a chapel. Above the main altar is a huge stone statue of Mary, without candles or flowers. Silent and focused, with soft folds in her grey marble gown.

I don't remember the first time I went to church. I know its name.

Saint Henry's. A low-ceilinged chapel beneath an elementary school. Candles were in metal stands, red ones by Jesus and the male saints. Blue ones by Mary and the female saints. Actually the candles were all white if you looked closely, but the glass containers holding the wax were colour and gender separated.

Now in the 1990s, some churches have plastic globes for candles. Red plastic bubbles with a black button that you push and an electronic wick appears at the feet of Jesus. But in the 1940s the candles were real and in glass containers and there was lace everywhere. On the edges of starched altar cloths. Priests' garments. Altar boys' sleeves. The edges of Mary's marble robe. Women's hankies. And the smell of frankincense lived in the air.

On winter Sundays, with the windows closed tight, this incense was overpowering. A mantle against every kind of madness, every kind of family. My family, a Lebanese father, a Scottish mother. One Catholic. One not. Each outcast by some of the other's side because each wasn't the other.

Fears or traumas of the 1940s were unmet. Peoples' needs were unattended in those days. No one questioned anything. Nothing was discussed. It was in this context, amid this wreckage, that I was born. A bastard child. Belonging to neither side completely. The people of my generation were born weighed down with the past.

All of us, angels with backpacks.

You could say anything when you prayed silently. Who could tell? And you could pray for as long as you wanted to within the time frame of the service.

My father's rosary would appear. I never saw those beads at any other time. He knelt with his black beads and I knelt beside him with something slightly more colourful.

The nuns sat in a divided-off area, singing the responses in Latin. We saw them only at communion, a long silent row of moving hearse-black fabric, a floor-length leather strap, and floor-length wooden rosary beads. The nuns who sang in Latin at Saint Henry's were the same nuns who taught in school, but in church they seemed other-worldly. Closer to God. It was confusing to go to the convent door in the morning on an errand and be greeted by a nun in an apron smelling of bacon and eggs.

The twelve years with the nuns lasted until 1961 and the future war in Vietnam. We prayed constantly, it seemed hourly, and from our little wooden desk with its ink-well we were trying to save the entire world from communism, savages, and anyone who wasn't Catholic, including my mother. No wonder I sat on the edge. The terror the nuns instilled in us is hard to make real. It seems as if it all happened in another century. Behind thick convent walls. The outskirts of a small medieval village. A bad movie in black and white. The nuns terrified store clerks, parents, and any plumber who had to fix a broken toilet. The nuns in the 1950s lived by ancient rules and so therefore did we. After a beating our hands would swell to what seemed like twice their size. I can still see the red. Hear the crack of a strap. Feel the sting.

The night the Chinese restaurant exploded, flames lit up the sky like something from a western movie. From our upstairs hall window, things made of wood were disappearing. Stunned families walked in rows, with clothes packed in a panic. Crying children pulled loaded wagons filled with stuffed pillowcases; photo albums with pictures of what their house used to look like. Men carried mattresses. Women held pots and pans. Where would the women use these pots? They had no stove now. They had no house. What should I save from possible ashes? Books. A stack of geography and arithmetic. If I didn't I'd be strapped. We'd all be strapped. Or kneel alone in the corner with index fingers to our lips. This was the worst! Our house escaped the flames but in the morning, streets were soaked with ashes, black water, and large cavities of smoldering sticks where yesterday there had been homes. This is why people carried the photo albums. If the fire was on a Tuesday, on Wednesday we walked to Saint Henry's chapel for weekly devotions, despite the weather, silently, across town, like little martyrs. Sister Mary Saint John the Baptist holding the only umbrella. If we spoke, the promise of a leather strap.

After devotions I'd visit my father in a store once owned by his father. A small dry goods store in a poor neighborhood. The entire town was mainly poor, so to own a store in a poor section was without much reward. Shoes were on display, one on top of the box, the other inside to discourage thieves. One day someone stole one shoe. We talked for months about that one stolen shoe. Basically, Wednesdays were a time for walking in silent obedience and for praying.

The only difference between the martyrs and us was that we didn't have holy cards with our pictures on them. Decades later I designed a large one for myself. In colour. Things slowly fell into place.

Everything eventually falls into place. Like a table setting. Like the orderly way we sat around the kitchen table in the late autumn of 1956 and listened to news about Hungary coming from the small black radio on the corner shelf. A wooden pyramid, flat on its back, holding up this burden of news. We didn't talk about it. We just listened to the reports of Soviet tanks mowing people down in the streets. Children holding their mothers' hands, mowed down. Men trying to protect their mothers, mowed down. And we ate our food. Everything was quiet except for the chewing. Everything seemed to be in black and white. War news followed by the soft voice of Elvis. "Love Me Tender."

Tanks crushing bodies. Love me. Tender.

There was something in Saint Henry's that was powerful. Hopeful. Something in the incense and candles and silent prayers. A moment when it was safe to stop the routine of whatever had become normal and speak silently to an invisible power. This is what my father believed. And it was his unshakeable belief, his rosary appearing for an hour every week, that led me on my search for churches in every city I ever lived in, ever spent more than a weekend in for the rest of my life.

We're shown the kitchen area. It's large and smells of lemons and muffins. Things are neat but in no particular order. Odd-sized glasses next to one another. Bowls peering out from other bowls, a mountain of straw baskets; a dishtowel is drying by an open window. Things are tidy but not rigid. A long wooden worktable is in the centre; a black-handled butcher knife to one side. My eye catches a brown old-fashioned radio on a shelf and my mind immediately flashes to another radio.

This radio knows nothing about Maritime radios in the 1950s— about reports from the fishery department, "gutted, head on," its reference to cod, followed by country and western music. At 10 A.M., Tchaikovsky, Piano Concerto No. 1 followed by shopping news, a contest sponsored by a soapsuds company, a clothing sale at the co-op store.

In winter, leaving the kitchen's warmth and walking to school through drifting snow, praying to God almighty that homework pages didn't get wet, because if they did and Sister Mary Whomever couldn't read it, it meant the leather strap in front of the class. Or outside in the dim hallway. It depended on the nun, they had individual styles.

Winter also meant rabbits would appear in the kitchen. Long wild carcasses caught in traps and brought into the house by men wearing heavy high-laced boots. These rabbit carcasses would be complete, the entire animal stretched out from ear to tail or paw-to-paw, however dead rabbits are measured, with drops of frozen blood from trying to pull themselves free, and puffs of fur torn in a struggle. The rabbits would have their legs cracked so they could fit into cooking dishes. It made a sound like someone cracking giant knuckles. The stomachs were sliced open down in the basement, over layers of paper and the entire fur removed, the head removed. Eventually these rabbits made their way upstairs, what was left of them, the broken bones and missing parts, the meat and bones, wrapped in newsprint to keep blood from dripping on the polished linoleum floor. The rabbits were packed into cooking dishes, with savory, and large heavy stitches holding flesh together, a darning needle and black thread. The rabbits were cooked and then we ate them.

I think pieces of those rabbits are inside me to this day. Wanting to escape. Wanting a chance to move away from a trap on a cold Newfoundland floor.

This is what we find ourselves wanting sometimes. A chance to move differently. A chance to move somewhere else instead.

A tiny elevator brings us to an open bookstore. A tin of coins lies in the centre of a small round table. In this building people are trusted to make their own change. Everything is unlocked once we get inside the main door with its code.

We are led down a dim hallway to a room where I am to spend the weekend. A birthday gift to myself, a weekend at an isolated retreat house that has been briefly described to me by my friend. Then return to Manhattan and the instability of my job. Dresser, theatre, the opera, and television shows; handing swords to anonymous people; starching petticoats. Sorting thousands of shoes. Quick changes in the dark. Turning ordinary people into beggars and queens. Creating magic through the illusion of costumes.

This retreat house, I am told, is thought to hold special powers or energy. No one knows how to describe it, or what in fact it is. People think it might have something to do with ley lines, invisible lines of power, connecting holy areas around the world. That it may be aligned with a sacred place somewhere, but no one knows anything for certain. I am shown where the extra blankets are.

I ask for a key, but there is none. None of the rooms have locks.

"It's just a bunch of nuns staying here," Sister Marie says.

Discussions and workshops are going to be held all weekend, she says, and I am welcome to participate. I smile and thank her but it's the last thing I want. I want silence. Want away from the sounds and images flooding my mind. I want to stand alone in the woods with trees.

The door won't close easily. It sticks. It's midnight and every sound echoes. But I keep working the door. I want at least that. I want the door shut.

My room is called *The Queen of Peace Room*. It's written on a narrow wooden plaque on the wall above the dresser. Below it a small mirror, just big enough so I can see myself from the neck up. The rest of me, apparently, doesn't exist here.

So with the presence of The Queen of Peace above me, I unpack for a two-day visit, clean clothes for the morning, herbal tea bags, hand cream, and holy cards.

Cool midnight air pours through the open window like oxygen or rain. Everything here is at peace. Leaves are resting on the shoulders of trees. Birds are sleeping in branches. In winter, with bare branches jutting into space, these birds would be as obvious as sunrise. No wonder they fly away. It isn't cold weather that makes them migrate. It's the lack of privacy. The wind feels like wide brushstrokes.

I light a candle in The Queen of Peace Room and make my usual altar on the bureau top—a thin blue scarf, pictures of angels, Gandhi, and Saint Dymphna, patron saint to keep one from going completely mad; a cardboard picture of Jiminy Cricket (a believer in faith and hope), and a Herkimer crystal.

A ribbon of incense smoke inches its way towards the scrubbed wooden windowsill. Moonlight falls on birch trees, a piece of altar lace waves in a breeze, sisters' t-shirts are drying on a clothesline. Stars are in place above every part of this complex, each one shimmering in the darkness.

I listen to the sounds of a bird, wind shifting leaves, the zing of crickets, and silence. Blue light spills across the bureau. This is the original magic.

Magic can't be destroyed. That's why it's called magic. The soft tick of the travel clock blends with the sounds of the night.

I look through The Queen of Peace window until I fall asleep.

Lea, (lē, lā), n. a grassland; a meadow.
— *The American Heritage Dictionary of the English Language,* Third Edition

Ley: the supposed line of a prehistoric track in a straight line usually from hilltop to hilltop with identifying points such as ponds, mounds, etc., marking its route.
— *Oxford English Dictionary*

Ley lines are mysterious energy channels that criss-cross the globe, and are more often than not to be found joining up two or three "sacred sites."
— Allen Robin, "A New Age Dawns for Science"

SATURDAY MORNING

I shower, dress, find the dining room, make a cup of tea, help myself to a few of the tiny muffins laid out on a sideboard, and wander upstairs to a sun-drenched room overlooking trees and an unpainted barn I hadn't seen last night. Trees are golden and lit by a sky of the same colour. Sunlight rests in branches like pieces from a broken mosaic. There's a cool breeze and silence except for the furious rapid song of a single robin. Then more birds, clear distinct sounds, like flute music. Sounds of flutes are coming from the trees. Maybe I should say this is all a dream and that would make it more believable.

But this is a dream:

One night I was a photograph, in black and white. Someone had a missing piece—a large ripped piece of paper torn from where my left arm would have been if the photo were complete. This arm fragment kept being passed among a group of people. I kept trying to reclaim it. But each time I got close, it was passed away from me, like a bird in flight. I moved faster and got closer. I could see the texture of the fragment. I almost touched it once, but then it vanished, like a shadow.

That was a dream. This is the truth: the entire landscape is shimmering.

Healthy plants are set upon tables the full length of the room. Lace curtains move in each breath of breeze. Large comfortable chairs are scattered about in a semi-orderly fashion, and around the windows, which run the full length of the room, are small wooden plaques with hand-carved inscriptions, photographs of nature, and paintings of birds.

Windows can be like clay in the hands of a potter, can be outlined with lace and geraniums. In churches, some windows are filled with colour and mysterious people telling a story; light spills through glass and rainbows appear on the face of a holy person, birds and angels seem to fly through a stained glass sky; windows can be broken and under the sea, tossed there from the back of a truck, fish darting through, coral attached to one side; they can be flung open and jumped through from the sixth floor of a city tenement by a dancer unable to dance again, who leaps instead to death; or jumped from by a wounded person, so hurt, so helpless, so angry that death through an open window becomes a passage to anywhere except here. Some windows can be so boarded shut, they may as well be plastered with cement, a wall now, instead of a window, never to be reopened. Windows can be the eyes of a soul, can be a thin wooden frame around a lost woman's face, looking through glass as if it were a mirror, having absolutely no concept of who she had been, or become, or where she is going.

I walk downstairs, outside, and stand in the cool wind and the smell of summer vegetation. I can see now that it's a complex of build-ings, a few barns, a large main wooden house with a wide veranda, and the brick structure where I've spent the night. A low stone-wall edged with birch and spruce surrounds everything. The only sounds are birds and crickets.

I walk along the paths surrounding the complex, then up the pris-tine wooded steps of the main house and can hear someone say, "All things that are supposed to meet will eventually meet."

In the large, lightly furnished room, people are seated in a circle, and there is a peacefulness I want to wrap myself in. There is gentle-ness, tremendous energy, and an unexpected warmth, like the top of a luncheonette counter on a winter morning, just after the orders to go have been picked up.

I listen to the voices, not the words themselves so much—but more to their gentle tone. They sound like nuns or angels. No, not nuns! Angels.

I have a pen but no paper. What am I thinking?

I fold a borrowed piece of paper and begin to take notes:

· What is a journey?

· The new voice you hear is often your own.

· Walk closely to the wise ones.

- Always ask questions.
- Pain happens to most of us.
- Get close to the earth.
- Get as close to the earth as possible.
- Protect each other's silence.
- Mountains can be moved.
- Listen to everything. Once.
- Learn to talk about simple things. Learn to talk about soup.
- Always go back to the journey.
- The dark side began for everyone.

The dark side began for everyone...my mind surges forwards and backwards, memories collide and overlap. I feel as if there isn't enough ink in the world for what I'd write, as if my knuckles are filled with ink. I find another pen and feel more secure. I am at the dawn of my fiftieth year, with nuns in the woods, and it's cold. I didn't bring enough socks.

We take a fifteen-minute coffee break and some of the women walk outside. Some have coffee and tiny muffins. Their hands are plain, and make almost no sound. My left thumbnail is splintered down the middle; two coats of nail polish still won't conceal it, caught in a car door when I was a child. It's never grown back properly. A reminder, not that I need one.

From the sun porch, which looks recently painted, I watch clouds swimming by, changing form, slowly and tenderly kissing. The sky finds room for all of them. There is never a cloud without a sky. They all belong and there's room for more. I place my own cloud there and watch it dissolve into a thousand different layers. The trees look up in amazement. They had no idea I was so complex. Only the sky knew and made room without question.

Everything changes form before the eyes of those who are looking up. The sky makes room gladly as seasons change below. Light changes too. It's the way it falls on things. Whole areas of trees are exposed. Parts of buildings become visible. Leaves fall and dark brown limbs jut into space, weightless, except for the light.

No matter where you are in the autumn, leaves fall and things that were once concealed are now exposed. In the summer, the woods fat with foliage, light is locked out. It was like this on the highways I remember in Newfoundland. It was like this at the cabin.

In winter, the cabin was picturesque, buried, and cold. In summer, it was alive with nature, isolation, and darkness. You had to walk up a hill to a little field to get sunlight.

The cabin was hand-built and rough. An icy brook for washing everything. There was no water in the house. Drinks were stored there, among fish that lived there. A duck swam by with her family in the spring. There was no electricity. There was no phone. There was no neighbourhood. This is where I washed before getting a ride to school with Bill, the egg deliveryman. At dawn. This was the 1950s. It feels like the 1850s with its isolation. The back room with its perishables and no refrigerator. We'd given these things up when we made the move to the woods. A move dictated by poverty.

On one side of the cabin was a large vegetable garden. Fenced off with wire to keep moose and deer away. One night deer attacked the garden and trampled the carefully planted rows. We all heard the noise. My father jumped from his bed in only his undershorts, out the cabin door, into the night and the broken yard and chased them up the road and onto the Trans-Canada Highway, like a crazed man in his underwear on the highway in the dark, running after deer. I don't know what he would have done if he'd caught one, if a deer had stumbled and my father was able to grab it by the face. The deer destroyed the garden and escaped and my father returned from the highway in his undershorts. And he may have been crying, but I couldn't see his face.

Down below on the unpaved road you'd never suspect the field existed. It was an enchanted area in the middle of a forest. I went there to get warm in tall stalks of golden grass. Is gold spun from straw or is straw spun from gold?

The field was bordered on all sides by trees. Clusters of spruce and birch and maple. Some of them misshapen because of the hard winters. But majestic in the sunlight despite their crooked backs and twisted limbs.

If you were in the field picking strawberries and the timing was just right, you could lift up the green leaves and the touch of your fingers would make the berry fall off its stem, right into your hand. Some of the berries needed to be pulled. They didn't give up the field easily. The white ones were left to mature. The ones that fell into my hand were my favourite. There was no struggle involved.

In the field, the embrace of light was everywhere and it was quiet as only light can be. It gave each leaf an identity. Rather, it confirmed the identity. Within minutes, everything would change. The light over everything was blue, like a thin cloak, like Picasso's blue period and one long streak of cloud would stretch across the sky like a highway. I wanted to walk on it. Take it wherever it was leading. Be its humble traveller. Quietly stepping on the softness. Staying within the boundaries of cloud road.

Light danced around a row of white cotton nightgowns hanging on a line outside a convent in France, outside a thousand quiet convents. I didn't see this but I know it happened. It made the gowns move gently, like the women who wore them. The light made the crème satin ribbons around the necks glisten like fine jewellery. It surrounded these garments worn in sleep, filled them with the light of light. It had been doing this for centuries, as long as convents and clotheslines have existed. These nightgowns were like holy skins of angels hung out to dry. Not like rabbit skins drying, violence pinning them in place as accurately as gunshot. These gowns were the quiet skins of angels, teardrops moving and filled with light.

There were two different highways and two different grandfathers. One was from the old country, Lebanon. A shopkeeper, a man who eventually became an invalid with a broken hip that wouldn't heal and spent his last years confined alone to a tiny dark room in a huge house that was otherwise sun-filled. I don't know his past. He always wanted water to wash his hands. It was like a ritual to him. Or maybe it seemed that way to me. It seemed religious. This was my father's father. I'd get him a pan of fresh water when we went to visit that small town. Botwood. Not even big enough to call a town. Whatever they call places before they become towns. Hamlets. He'd pray in his narrow dark room and wash his hands, with light everywhere else in the house except near him, as if he were being forced to die before his time. Light deprivation. A wife who didn't love him. A mail-order bride at fifteen, finally in control of things. A giant slab of watermelon near her sunny bed, a butcher knife piercing its flesh.

Then there was the other grandfather. The one I want to forget but can't. The man with the large hands for chopping wood, splitting logs open, and splitting other things open too.

This is not a fairy tale.

It has to do with a lake. Driving there on summer Sundays. When our car reached the place on the highway where the house was, down at the bottom of a large pasture, everyone would leave except my grandfather and me. I was young. Seven or eight. My grandfather said his leg was bad. So my parents decided that I was to stay in the car and keep him company. This is what I had to do on Sunday afternoons. To be quiet and to keep him company.

The front seat of the car was silent. Everything was silent. We sat next to one another, him on the passenger side. Me in the middle part. I think the seat was covered with plastic, washable.

Around us, and in some cases touching the windows, were thousands of trees. Nothing but spruce and birch and maple. I don't remember hearing birds. They may have been there but I don't remember them. Birds of prey don't sing.

The highway at that time was unpaved and when an occasional car whizzed by, a cloud of brown dust settled on the windows like curtains. This grandfather had a glass eye and sometimes he'd remove it while he and I were alone, and place it on the dashboard. An eyeball staring back at me. At the two of us. I was told to be quiet. Not to tell anyone about anything. In this solitude of spruce and birch and maple, this grandfather would remove my clothing and put his hands inside me, silently looking straight ahead, except for the eyeball resting on the dashboard. I looked straight ahead too, through the dirty car window, up to the sky.

The car radio was never on. Silence.

There's more to this story but I don't know if I'm able to write it. The pen I need is red like a cinder that's been smoldering for almost half a century. It wants to write the evil of this man. His hands doing things they never should have done. It wants to write the feelings of total child abandonment, beginning with Saturday nights. Knowing Sunday was next and the car ride up there and knowing what was to come, and asking if I could go down to the picnic with everyone else but being refused. This happened several times. Everything happened several times. Everything was silent. Windows rolled up tight.

Needing to go to the bathroom and being taken out of the car, across the unpaved highway. Not being allowed to go down to the house. Being taken up an embankment and into a woodsy part of the forest. I remember the birch trees. There I would squat, Sunday dress up around my shoulders, while he stood behind me, staring at me in that position, and he picked leaves for me to wipe myself. He'd stare at me for a long time before handing me a leaf, the forest now rubbing against the hurting parts of my child body. Then we'd silently return to the car and just stare ahead, through the dusty windshield. At least this is what I did. I didn't look at him, both eyes inside his head by now. I just stared ahead.

I've always wondered why, in all those Sundays that summer, never once did anyone ever come up from the big house to see if I wanted anything. A sandwich or a glass of water.

The vivid dreams began in the cabin. My bedroom. Next to the unfinished back room with hard-backed beetles falling to the floor. They sounded like ballpoint pens falling. Ballpoint pens in the middle of the night. I would dream of being captured by strangers who were always on horseback outside the back room. I'd run to the front door in these silent dreams. Even my dreams were silent, like silent movies. I'd run through the cabin to the front door but there'd be more strangers, tall, on horseback, waiting.

This was a recurring nightmare all through the years we lived up the highway. That's what away from the city meant. *Up the highway*. It was never indicated how far up. It was as if you'd disappeared. You were now *up the highway*, like *laid to rest* or *overseas*. Something that broad and vague.

I'd wake up fast and hard, like something had slapped me. Sometimes crying. And if my father were home, he'd come in from the other bedroom with a flashlight or a kerosene lamp and sit with me.

In the autumn on the way to school I'd pray for the car to crash. An accident. Taking me. I couldn't stand any more humiliation, any more hands inside me. Better for the damn car to crash. I was ready to die. How long does a person have to live anyway? Crash car. Crash. Dear sweet Jesus, please make the car crash.

I tried to get away from the little girl sitting on the front seat of that car, looking through the dusty window. I tried to get away from the girl sitting silent, staring straight ahead, with the old man next to her, looking wherever he was looking. I tried to get away from the little girl in that car, sitting abandoned, betrayed, isolated, her lower body parts aching. I tried to get away from her all of my life, but it was useless. Her large eyes would be forever staring back at me through so many afternoons as I sat there in silence. Trying to see the sky. Listening for the people who never came. Trying to figure out what I had done, who I had done it to, when I had done it. What was it that I had done in this short life to cause me to be in this situation? I tried to get away from it, to run from it in my mind, but her eyes would stare back at me for the rest of my life. And the eyes were haunting and unrelenting.

There is a stillness that exists sometimes around 5 A.M., a peace that has settled on buildings and trees during the night. And the further away you get from the city, the longer this calm lasts, until, if you get far enough, stillness lingers on the trees and ground from sunrise to sunrise. From season to season.

This calmness didn't exist on the trees near the car where my grandfather sat. Where I sat next to him.

NO!

He was sitting next to me. I was NEVER sitting next to him.

This stillness and peace didn't exist on the trees there. In that part of the Newfoundland forest, the trees were screaming. They made loud piercing sounds. They doubled over in pain. They threw up. They held on to each other in fear and disbelief. They pulled themselves up from their roots, throwing up as they ran. And the smell of their vomit permeated the forest. A family that permits child abuse is a suicidal family.

I sit on the porch with the shadows of these serene women criss-crossing around me.

If only we learned to love one another as carefully as we learn to drive. Obtain a license, I.D. cards with pictures, proving that we've passed an exam. We can now love. Without harm.

When we touch each other, we are touching each other's past.

The arms of a family are how we see love. If those arms aren't there, for whatever reason, it's difficult to have a sense of self.

We return to the large room and people speak about their personal life journeys. Where they've come from, where they are going. I mention a little about my grandfather. Grand should be removed from his name. Replace it with something else. Two of the sisters have been sexually abused as children, little is said, only the statement in itself.

We speak and take notes until almost noon, then pray silently and privately over our macaroni. I remember a prayer we used to chant as children when we were away from the nuns, "Holy Mary Mother of God, Send Me Down a Fishing Rod!" But I don't say this prayer out loud. I just remember it.

I'm not sure if I'm with witches, angels, saints, or nuns. I am sure of only one thing. I am with wise women in an isolated area in the woods, and I have one new scribbled note: "To complete the journey, you must first slow down and look around, to see where you are." There is no calm anywhere, except at this complex.

Nothing is scheduled after lunch. People are free to walk in the woods, relax in a meadow at the bottom of the hill in front of the meeting house, read, have tea and cookies, or swim in the pool, or all of it. I decide to do everything except swim in the pool, being unable to swim, but spend most of the day in the meadow.

The meadow is actually two meadows. As if it has been divided exactly in half by an invisible line or energy. As if one is the body and one is the mind.

The upper half is mowed close and bordered on three sides by trees, bushes, and some kind of red, wild, climbing berries. A wooden shrine to the Crucifixion is off to one side, partially hidden with overgrowth, a very private, personal area in the woods. The fourth side is actually a cliff that leads down to a lower wild meadow. A green wooden bench in the middle of the upper meadow overlooks everything.

The lower meadow is left as nature created it. Nothing sets foot there except wild creatures; it is an expanse of tall wild grass and high golden reeds which, at a distance, in the sunlight, make it look like a lake of liquid gold. Everything is bordered by towering trees. This is where I spend most of the afternoon. At the fringe of wildness.

In the late afternoon, light touches every part of the complex and windows blush pink.

At 6 P.M. we say quiet, private thanks over supper, heads bow momentarily over pasta, salad, chocolate pudding, and coffee. Almost institutional food but by calling it pasta I change it.

Evening walks quickly towards the complex. Things are put away. Voices are barely a whisper. A moon appears in a cloudless sky. Women walk softly on the shadows of trees. Then a quiet evening prayer in candlelight on the veranda, a prayer for the earth, for a peaceful night, then a moment of quiet.

One completed day.

In the California Sierras, the prehistoric Miwok Indians left behind the remains of dead-straight tracks.

— Paul Devereux, *The Long Trip*

Newfoundland tradition is that you must "wet a line" on Queen Victoria's birthday. It marks the beginning of the trek to the summer homes and cottages in Newfoundland.

— Alice Lannon and Mike McCarthy,
*Fables, Fairies and Folklore of
Newfoundland*

SUNDAY, 7 A.M.

I wash, dress, and say a quick prayer at my make-shift altar. I didn't sleep under the blankets, so I don't have to make my bed. This is a bonus time-wise.

We meet in the upper meadow and meditate as we face each of the four directions. Then hold hands as we face the centre and one another. These women are all ages, all kinds, and all kind. A woman reads the poetry of Rumi, "There are hundreds of ways to kneel and kiss the ground."

Clouds shift and everything turns momentarily to shades of rose and mauve. This meadow is a balm. A painting too large for any canvas. Women sit on the grass, in silence. Each person's mind is focused inward, so there is space, peace.

A tree with crooked branches stretches into the morning air. This tree doesn't care if anyone thinks it's beautiful. It breathes anyway. One branch juts precariously, not crowded together with the others, connected but with space, unable to grow without space. Tiny leaves fall to the ground, like soft feathers that cover the heart area of a bird.

Each woman leaves the meadow slowly, each at her own pace.

After a brief mass in the chapel, we walk to the dining room. I bypass the scrambled eggs and bacon and eat home fries and melon instead. As much as I want, of both. There's also cereal, muffins, and juice. My eyes are bigger than my stomach. And they remember too much. The year we ate canned corned beef from Australia. The years of nothing.

"Just say you've eaten," is what my mother would say. "Just say you've eaten." So with a potato or egg or something, there was always something, we'd wait for my father to come home, put his coat away, and his plastic overshoes, his rubbers if it was raining or muddy. We called them rubbers. It had nothing to do with safe sex or the plague, which was to strike the later part of the century.

He'd place his rubbers on carefully folded newspapers, roll his shirt sleeves above his elbows, remove his gold watch with the expansion band, and place it on the windowsill above the kitchen sink. The window overlooked a rock garden and a row of dahlias that my mother had planted. He'd lather his hands and arms, rinse, dry, and sit at the table. Then he'd make the sign of the cross over himself. He did this before and after every meal. Settle into his aluminum chair. And my mother would serve him a meal of meat. Fish if it was Friday. And vegetables. And a salad, usually cucumber with the green peel on the outside of the white, sliced tomatoes with little specks of black pepper sprinkled on top, and lettuce or celery with the delicate leaves still attached to the heart pieces of the stalk. Sometimes black olives. And always a plate of bread and butter. And he would look at me, sitting rigid in my chair, dangerously close to the edge, ready to go into flight, and he'd say, "Where's your supper?"

And I'd say, "I've already eaten. I've already eaten." And my mother would sit at her end of the table, silently holding a lit cigarette and my father would begin to eat his meal. A big meal. On Sundays we all ate the same. There was no way around this on Sundays. Harp music on the radio. Pat Boone, "April Love."

Inside the skin is self. Outside is non-self. Where I began, and where others, by their actions, were telling me I began, was vague. Sexual, physical, and emotional abuses are violations of personal boundaries. Problems arise when boundaries are not respected. The years without food were the years of furniture against doors. High bureaus and heavy stuffed chairs pushed tight into place. Blinds pulled down, curtains pulled tight with safety pins, and my mother huddled in a state beyond fear in one corner of the bedroom she'd locked us all in, with a tin pot in case we needed to do that. My baby sister, two young cousins, and me. Four small children there to protect her against invisible demons. Maybe something had terrified her in the past and lingered. When my father was working as a travelling salesman, our house was engulfed at night with the horror of invisible demons, seen only by my mother.

It was from one of the kitchen chairs that I passed out for the first time. I'd been getting dizzy and weak for years. Once I'd been walked home from church by a neighbour. But nothing was ever mentioned. It was ignored, as if it had happened to another person, in another household.

It was late spring or early summer. Probably both. I'd planted nasturtium seeds around the steps leading up to the back door. Nasturtium seeds are big and hardy and strong looking and this type of seed appealed to me at the time. Sometimes we want a strength that's on our side. I passed out. An arm's length from the nasturtium seeds.

Just as a machine knows when it's overloaded, so does the brain. Abuse and silent images were mounting and blurring—and the body finds a coping mechanism. It shuts down. Given sufficient stress, each body will collapse into a seizure. There is no mystery involved.

I'd just started a summer job and was planning to leave Newfoundland to study. My year book said: "Ambition: Interior Designer." I'd met an interior designer. She spoke calmly, without stumbling all over her words. I wanted to be that.

There were too many experiences inside my brain, they were colliding, and I passed out cold, on the kitchen floor, like one of the winter rabbits.

I was taken to a hospital after the second time I lost consciousness.

"Your father tells me you're a very nervous person," the doctor said.

"I'm not nervous," I said.

My fingernails were slicing through the knotted hands he couldn't see from behind his wooden desk. I'd been getting dizzy and falling for years but no one talked about it. As if there were two of me, the one who fell and the one who didn't.

Seizures can be caused by any number of things—incest, food deprivation, severe stress and shock, rape, marital abuse, abandonment. They're a tiny charge of electricity in the brain, causing a change in how a person feels. Seizures can be triggered by electrical storms inside the mind of a person who has been touched by madness and is attempting to remain calm. They aren't punishment because the person was a shit in a past life. Seizures happen, like weather, like spring. They're aggravated by stress and poor living habits. The absence of food can manifest itself in all kinds of ways.

At eighteen I left with a three-piece set of white luggage, and a blood-red lining, carrying a wall as wide as pain around me. In the 1960s, people with epilepsy were denied entry into the United States. I had to lie to get into art school. My father mailed medication. I'd been told to be silent and I obeyed.

Epilepsy. I look at the word on the page and it becomes a green demon covered with warts.

1964. I didn't realize the United States was at the brink of war. Maybe war seemed normal to me. I wrote poems about death, and burning villages, and blood, and screamed them through Manhattan microphones. I became a member of the peace movement. But was unable to speak about the unbearable pain in my own heart. If I did I'd break open.

Somewhere, between the geography of the meadow and the complex itself, the layers of my past are unravelling, and nothing can stop it. The thoughts and images I've buried for years are rushing to the surface, wanting to be free. There is something in the landscape of this retreat house, maybe the land itself, an ability to connect with the power of the ground and the liquid gold alchemy of the meadow.

It had never been my intention to attend any of these discussions. It had been my intention to walk alone, quietly, in the woods for two days. To stand in the silence of trees. Then return to New York.

Most of the sisters are strangers to one another, arriving at the complex individually for a week-long retreat from locations across North America. But in a very short span of time, we've given each other unconditional permission to speak about anything, to think about anything.

We wander in the meadow, share meals, meditate in sunrise and moonlight, listen intently to each other's stories, walk through forests alone and together, pray together, laugh out loud in the middle of the woods.

By Sunday evening, two things are certain. One, I am convinced that some part of my life is here to be examined and reclaimed. And two, I am scheduled to leave in the morning.

At 9 P.M. I go for peach ice cream with some of the women to a nearby town. Peach, flavour and colour. Two things in one.

We return to the complex. The meadow. The monastery. I walk back to our hallway. Our hallway. Not mine or theirs. Ours.

I feel as if I belong with these strangers. As if there is work to be completed.

One looks at me gently as she begins to close her door. She puts her finger to her head, where her brain is. Her brain, not mine with its defect.

"Think" she says, "Just think."

Think, I think to myself. And we say goodnight.

I want to go back to her room. Pound on the door and say, "Hold me. Just hold me. That's all I've ever wanted. Someone to hold me."

But she's a nun for god's sake and I don't even know her last name. Her door clicks shut, gently. Everything these women do is gentle. I walk back to The Queen of Peace Room. Light a candle, look out the window, eat the piece of fruit I'm not supposed to have in my room, write, listen to a tape of medieval songs on my walkman, change into my white cotton nightgown, put cream on my face and hands and legs and write more.

It's midnight. And I can't sleep. I get dressed again, blow out the candle, put on a double layer of shirts, walk from the building into total darkness, and prepare to walk down to the meadow, through thick blackness. The hill seems much steeper in the dark and the grass is slippery with dew.

Midnight again, and feeling my way through darkness, one guarded footstep after another. Head bent downward. A walking meditation in the dark.

I can make out shapes. The long clump of berry bushes with thorns and the Crucifixion is to the right. The wild deepest part of the meadow and the ledge are directly in front of me. The uncleared woods are to the left. The complex of buildings is behind me. It's the fringe of the meadow that I'm looking for. And the green wooden bench, overlooking through tall grass, the large wild meadow. I want to sit there, at the fringe. And think.

My foot comes in contact with a solid object. In the pitch darkness I've found the bench and slide onto it. There are three things in front of me. At the very bottom of the darkness, mountains, trees, and ground all meet. Directly above that are huge bands of amber-coloured glow. It covers entire areas of sky, from east to west. And north to south. These amber-coloured, pink/brown/gold-coloured bands (there is no name for this colour); these bands of light simply exist. They do nothing except glow, everywhere, over the meadow, the wild field, and everything within it.

Light. The memory of. The sun, the moon, a candle. To stand in one's own light. Christmas lights anywhere. Light outdoors as snow falls in the evening. Early morning light through trees in a campground. Or on a beach. Light and how it changes everything. Embraces everything. The memory of light is complex, like the buildings behind me, and multifaceted. I think about light for what seems like hours. What it does to trees. To the sky. The rainbows it makes as it passes through crystals hanging in a window.

Directly above me are two large unblinking stars. Like eyes or opals.

The eyes of night are staring at me. We have finally met. Me and the night.

I look into the eyes of darkness and there is only beauty and wonder. Nothing to fear. I look at the bands of light, expecting all kinds of things to happen. I expect large images of stern religious figures to come walking out of the clouds. Planets to come zooming towards me. But nothing happens. The bands of colour simply exist, glowing. I tilt my head further up, and it seems as if there is no darkness. There are so many stars, they outnumber the sky. Two distinct colours, gold and silver, next to one another. If this were a painting in progress I would say to the artist, "You have too many stars there. You've gone a little too far." But it isn't a painting. Stars are bursting through the darkness.

I sit on the wooden bench alone. But how can I say in the dark.

So much is now in the past. I am away from all the knives at all the different places. Away from so much madness. Away from Thirteenth Street on the Lower East Side. Away from that night.

Overhead, a bird flies so high it is almost invisible. Now I know why some birds fly so high.

What happened on Thirteenth Street was not considered an official rape.

The Vietnam War was in full swing. By now, the pictures of boys coming across the screen in body bags, images that today are historical footage, were, at that time, simply what one saw when the news was turned on. Artists and poets were writing and creating their brains out, and some were blowing their brains out. I'd been writing poetry for about eight years. Some of it god-awful stuff in high school. Pieces I took quite seriously because they captured the activity in my mind and a local parish priest offered to read them. I'd knock on the rectory door, wait for an inside hall light to shine through the small frosted glass window, and then a priest or one of those women who worked in the homes of priests, cooking and cleaning, would appear. I delivered my parcel of words, and days later, maybe weeks, whenever our paths crossed again, he told me that he'd read my poems and liked my writing. Then I put together another parcel, delivered them and he told me weeks later the same thing. I never got these poems back. He never returned them and I was too embarrassed to ask for them. So this entire body of work, mostly about trees and visions and the weather, is dead. I secretly like to think they're buried in some vault in the Vatican, these nature poems, to be discovered one day, when restorations are made to some part of Rome. But I know better.

They were my first poems.

The next series was not so genteel. They were about blood and war and death and looking the other way. The way my grandfather used to look in that car years earlier.

These poems, the second group, were read nightly, at coffee shops and colleges and churches. Poets coming together, to read, to educate, to inform, to get a message out to the world, while we still had a world.

Trying to educate was common, especially in the mid-60s. By the end of the decade we were all so tired we didn't know who we were. In 1970 peace demonstrators were shot dead at Kent State.

But this was the mid-60s and we had a lot of strength. And hope.

The hour was late.

I say this because many people say what happened was my own fault because of the hour.

I was in a neighbourhood that was a little rough. Thirteenth Street on the Lower East Side. I'd lived there for awhile and knew the blocks pretty well, but it could be rough if you were an outsider. And I was alone, coming home from the latest anti-war poetry reading.

I tell you these things so that you will have enough information to blame me, if you feel so inclined. Personally, I don't give a damn. I have taken it from both sides. From those who have me directly responsible because it was late and I was alone on a somewhat rough street. A woman didn't do these things in the 60s. Women are still not doing it. I wonder when women will be able to walk down a street, alone, at night, and not be attacked.

So, against this background, late, alone, and on a somewhat rough street, I left the coffee shop, walked the half block to the corner, made a right and prepared to walk the two blocks to my apartment.

I say prepared, because there's a certain amount of preparation that's done in walking the streets alone. By a woman anyway. You look for rowdy drunks. Your eyes do that sweeping search of the entire street as you round a corner. One fast sweeping movement to catch sight of anything that looks unusual. A fight. A car being robbed. A bust. A loud lovers' quarrel. Someone throwing things from a window. A crazy walking dangerously fast, dangerously close. These are things I just do automatically whenever I turn a corner. No one taught me this. It's just something I do. Have always done since I've lived in big cities. To be on the lookout.

In the country I watch for other things. I watch for the indentations of animals' bodies in high grass. Grass bent down during the night while the animal slept. Maybe with its young tucked around its warm body. I watch for these broken grass indentations and I know that large animals are likely nearby and so I'm cautious. Not fearful. But I proceed with slowness, not to alarm them.

I listen to the birds. The further away you get from trees, the harder it is to hear the birds. In a large open field, treeless, the sounds of birds are faint. You have to really listen. It's as if this is the hunting ground for butterflies and crickets and things that live on the stalks of high grass or beneath it. This area is too delicate for birds. This is where wild animals sleep during the night and the brilliant blue and black butterflies live by day. Dragonflies and thin, delicate creatures. In the country also, if you're lucky, you can see entire families of deer, quietly having dinner, one eye on the ground and one eye always on the lookout.

And so, this is how I turned the corner, that late night. One eye on my bulging, dangerous manuscript and one eye on Thirteenth Street.

I'd walked about three quarters of the distance to my apartment building when a man in a navy pea jacket, large black buttons shining in the dark, appeared about half a block in front of me.

He was walking very fast. I stepped a little to my left or my right, I can't remember which, but I stepped out of his path. I was guessing he had a path and at the same time I looked quickly to see what was around me. Four men were fighting over a bottle of wine outside an all-night bodega. Not a comforting option, if I found myself needing one, I thought. By now this man in the navy pea jacket was in front of me and before I had time to think, to do anything, he whacked me across the side of my neck and knocked me against the side of a parked car.

People actually parked cars on these streets. With belongings in them. This was before all the cute bumper stickers that read "EVERY-THING STOLEN ALREADY" and "NO RADIO INSIDE."

He whacked me fast and hard against the right side of my neck, then one more blow across the face, covering the lips. I dropped my head on the hood of a parked car. My head was whirling as he grunted and walked away from me as if in disgust. This happened in front of the stairs that led up to my apartment building. I straightened up from the hood of the car, put one hand to my head, clutching my manuscript with my other hand. With a really tight grip I'd learned on the bar frame of a crib. Hold on. Don't let the forces knock you down. I pulled myself away from the hood of the car, manuscript in one hand, other hand to my head and looked up the street where this man in the navy pea jacket had rushed and I saw him running back towards me.

I remember it in different parts of my body differently. I ran for my steps and ran as fast as I could up the crooked stoop into the unlocked front door.

In the 60s it wasn't unusual to have apartment houses with unlocked front doors. There were buildings with locked front doors, but it was about half and half at this point.

I ran in through the front door and began to climb the steps to my sixth-floor apartment.

I remember my legs separately from me, almost like long wings with shoes. I remember him running behind me. I seemed to be running but not moving really. His footsteps were gaining.

I landed on the sixth floor and fumbled for my keys in my bag.

You can blame me for this too.

If a woman does go out late at night and does walk home alone, she should have her keys in her hands at all times.

I didn't.

I had my manuscript. My bulging manuscript of poems about the Vietnam War and the United States government and burning villages.

My hands couldn't find the keys fast enough. When they finally did, when I finally got my fingers on these metal keys, it was too late. He was already on the sixth-floor landing, walking towards me in his navy pea jacket with its black shiny buttons with the anchors carved into them. He walked towards me holding an opened silver knife in his right hand. I remember the hand.

"Don't you scream," he said, "Don't you scream."

My keys were in the door.

"Do you live here alone?" he said. I wanted to say so many things. My mind raced. My legs were turning into water beneath me. I could literally feel my knees knocking. He held the knife to my face and asked me again, "Do you live here alone?"

I said "Yes."

I could feel my mind beginning to leave. Something or someone else was beginning to take over. To handle this situation with me. My body was trembling far too much to be speaking or thinking this rational.

"What do you want," I said. "Get out of here."

With the knife still at my head, he pushed the door open with his other hand and pushed me inside.

He said he wanted a glass of water and to leave the lights turned off.

It was common back then to have those white candles that come in glasses. They lasted for days and were more efficient than regular candles because you could use the glass containers for other things. To hold pens and pencils. To put flowers in. To hold loose change. He said he wanted a glass of water and I reached in the dark, by the sink, and poured water into a glass. I thought that's what I did. It turned out to be a glass in which the candle had burned low. I didn't know this in my nervousness.

I handed him this glass with the wax still inside and in the dark he realized it and threw the water in my face.

My legs continued shaking out of control. I don't know how they were still holding me up. It was a memory called forward, like retrieving something on a computer. This is how not to fall down, the body says. And sometimes it is successful.

He pushed me into the living room and on top of a sofa and jumped on top of me. My face was still wet with the water from the candle glass.

I screamed I was pregnant. It wasn't true. But I screamed it anyway. I thought that might stop him. My fear at this point was the knife.

My mind was working like that news band, that electronic news band that flashes non-stop in Times Square. This is what's happening now…this is what's happening now…this is what's happening now. Just a steady stream of facts.

I am in the dark.

I am alone with a rapist.

I am with a man who has a silver knife to my head. There is no chance that anyone will be in this apartment except the two of us.

What is the worst possible thing that can happen?

It flashes on the electronic band, whirling around the Times Square of my mind.

What is the worst thing that can happen?

He can kill me and throw me out the sixth-storey open window.

When there were no fire escapes coming across the path of windows, we left the windows open for air. A summer breeze. That's why the window was open. My mind flashed to the window in the front seat of the car with my grandfather. But this was different. This involved a silver knife, which was pointed at my head and the sixth-floor window, which was open.

"I'm pregnant," I said, "You're hurting me. You're hurting my stomach." I thought this might make him go away. He said he'd be real gentle. But I said I had to get up. I was getting sick.

I couldn't control my arms and legs. They seemed like limbs belonging to a rubber doll. They kept shaking. I leaned against a chair. He walked towards me with the knife to my neck, "If anyone walks in, you get it first," he said.

I'd dealt with all this before but they'd all been separate. I'd dealt with being sexually attacked. I'd dealt with knives in my face, bigger ones, butcher knives. With being terrorized in the dark. But they were all at separate times. Different years. This was all happening at the same time. This was hard. This was really hard.

I leaned against a chair and tried to breathe. He had funny eyes and I could see them in the darkness. Then he wanted to talk. With the silver knife to my face, he started talking about his drug habit, his friends, his mother. His eyes were dilated from drugs. He was not going to be rational for a long time. He talked about his women. His weapons. This one-sided surrealistic conversation in the dark occurred at knifepoint, by an open window, on the sixth floor.

Then he told me to light a candle and hold it to his face. He said he wanted me to remember him. I didn't ask why. I got a candle. I don't remember if it was the same candle glass that I'd put water in earlier or another one. I lit the candle and thought of throwing the fire in his face but was afraid I'd miss. I held the candle to his face, as ordered, but I saw nothing. Only darkness.

My shaking legs bent under me. I put the candle on a table and fell to the kitchen floor. I passed out. Just like I'd fallen to the kitchen floor in another house at another time. The body finds a way to cope. A coping mechanism. My brain was overloaded. The electrical system controlling all these messages was defective.

I fell to the floor. But somehow I remained aware. On some level.

I don't remember being carried to the bed. I just remember finding myself there, feeling him open my clothes, touching me, and putting his body next to mine. My eyes were closed tight. My brain seemed to be closed tight. Something else was in control, something else was making me function. Although I didn't have much to do. I was just lying on the bed. Silent. Still. Eyes closed. As if I were dead.

He put parts of his naked body next to mine. His penis seemed to be near my stomach a lot. I remember this. Maybe he thought he was fucking my imaginary baby. Maybe this was his pleasure. My mind felt complete penetration. A word I found out later, the police would like to use often.

I remember his breathing. And I remember worrying about the knife and the sixth-floor window. This level of consciousness that I found myself in was new. I was trying to save my own life from outside my life. I was watching all of this from a distance. Whatever was being done to my body was secondary. What would happen to my life was more important. I didn't want this to be the final chapter. I didn't want my throat slashed and to be found curled in a heap at the bottom of a tenement building by children on their way to school in the morning. I didn't want to be stabbed to death.

I didn't want to end up like those rabbits that were ripped open in the basement at home, with their legs broken so they could fit into cooking dishes.

I lay on the bed, silent and unmoving, my eyes tightly closed.

When he was finished he got off me, walked somewhere else in the apartment and I heard the door close. But I didn't know for sure if he'd really gone. If it was a trick. If I'd open my eyes and find him staring over me, grinning, with the silver knife in his hand.

I lay on that bed, motionless, for what seemed like half a day. It was probably three or four hours. But it seemed like half a day. I listened for his breathing. I listened for his footsteps.

I listened to every single sound that god ever created.

I watched for daylight through closed eyelids. I listened until I was sure he'd left the apartment. And then I very slowly opened my eyes.

Where I had in fact been during this time, this night, I don't know. I know I was in the apartment. But I'm also certain my mind was somewhere else. Outside of my body. Off to the side. Coping.

After my eyes were open, I waited a long time before I moved. I was like an animal. I felt like an animal. I looked like an animal. A mauled animal.

I finally got up, walked to the door, and locked it after I was sure the apartment was empty. Waited several hours. Then went to a friend for help.

A week later I went back to the apartment for my belongings. I went with the two toughest, biggest, tallest, strongest men I knew. One on each side of me.

I walked towards the steps of my building and in the shadows, in his navy pea jacket, he was waiting and watching. He was there again. How long had he been there?

My body froze. The only thing that worked was my voice. So I screamed and screamed and screamed.

Things began to move very quickly.

The navy pea jacket ran into a stream of moving traffic, with a tough big man behind him. The other man stayed with me.

A police car whaled alongside the curb and the siren matched the sounds coming out of my throat.

The police were a joke. This was the 1960s. Before sensitivity training. Before feminism and female cops.

"When did he take his penis out, miss?"

"How far in did he put it, miss?"

This is what they were asking me on that October night as I shook under a siren and held onto the straps in the back seat of the speeding police car so I didn't fall over.

At the station my hands wouldn't stop shaking.

"Try to get a hold of yourself, miss."

"Do you have a nervous disorder?" a cop asked.

YES! I wanted to say. My brain doesn't work properly. I can be a very nervous person. My brain is broken. I will never be the same. I'm a defect.

"No," I said.

I was put inside a room like a cage. Alone. Wire covered the windows. And given a huge album of New York City rapists. And told to let them know, outside, if anyone looked familiar.

I actually looked at these pictures. Black and white glossy images. My mind was blind. It saw nothing. I told them no. No one looked familiar.

This was not considered an official rape by the police department. Penetration wasn't deep enough.

Looking back on it now, I realize no one ever mentioned attempted murder!

The police were concerned only with the depth of penetration. Rape is measured according to the distance a man's penis travels.

I heard one cop say to another, "Just the usual rape, Charlie." And I was given a business card with a phone number to call if I was stalked or attacked again.

I carried that card with me for a long time, just as a reminder of how things are measured.

I never went inside the apartment building again. Friends moved my belongings. I found a new apartment. My white luggage with its blood-red lining moved. Again.

Like a town map, my body was being divided into sections. My mind divided it. My body was the land. My mind established the boundaries. And they were everywhere.

This was like war. I was the battleground.

I tried to take a bath but the water was filled with fish. Some of them were dead, floating belly-side up, to the top of the tub. The navy washcloth turned into a person. An injured person and drowned. Sank to the bottom. The glycerine soap slid out of my hand and sank— also—drowned. The fish kept dying. I pulled the plug. The water drained. Everything disappeared, except for the limp washcloth. Navy. And my memories.

I tried to sleep but I didn't feel safe. I wanted to place my hand over my entire body, apply heat like one would place a hand over an ice cube, and with enough steady pressure feel the ice cube melt. I wanted to do this to the walls I felt rising around me. Rising within me. But I was exhausted.

My eyes finally closed and I dreamt.

There were two horses. One horse was lying on the ground with a group of people standing around it. The horse was having its stomach cut open. The other horse was having parts of its body removed. Mutilated. Neither horse was dead. They both looked like human beings more than horses. Then there was intense anger on the part of the people standing around. This anger was directed at the people who'd caused the mutilation. But no one did anything.

Time passes quickly. I'm at a huge outdoor theatre in this dream. A performer is on stage. The performer is covered in robes and jewels. Somehow, without any words being said, I knew that the jewelled, costumed performer on stage was one of the horses. The performer resembled grace and pride combined with deformity. Somehow all feelings were understood without words.

Then I saw a darkness that seemed to have great depth. And I heard two things distinctly. One was the rolling of a great body of water, like waves splashing back and forth or a hand swishing water in circles. The second sound terrified me. A choir of angels, humming close to me. The combination of darkness, strange-sounding water, and close voices singing terrified me. I literally shook myself awake. Thought I was seeing my own death.

I went back to sleep. Almost immediately a similar event took place.

I became extremely nervous and shook myself awake again. I was afraid of leaving my physical body. I stayed awake.

I needed energy that was stronger than ever before.

What was happening underneath the skin? Near my heart. My soul. I heard rain. Inside me. A driving, pounding rain. I never wanted to go outside again. I became angry at my own impatience. With the uneasy quiet. I wanted to run through it like a field. To race through this silence of question marks and get to the other side where the answers were. But it seemed I was alone and I'd been alone enough. On this one I wanted a companion. To repair the damage I was about to repair, I needed someone beside me. Someone besides me.

But there was only one answer. Wait. I looked at the sky instead. In silence. Wait. Listen. Above all, trust.

I put down the things I'd been holding onto and watched the sky through an open window.

This went on for weeks.

I counted the cracks in the plaster. I counted the drips of blood from the faucet. Or was it water. I counted the times people went up the stairs and down the stairs.

Counting calmed me.

And through all of this the sky stayed with me. Never once leaving. Never once having anywhere else to go. Whenever I woke up, it would be there. And in time I felt the weight of things fall away.

Some of it.

On Thanksgiving I went into a tailspin of depression and flashbacks and attempted suicide with pills. White codeine. From a corner drugstore. I'd given myself a month to get over it for Christ's sake. How much time did I need?

Two Jamaican poets, who knew me well, climbed the back fire escape and broke the locked apartment window. The same men who'd walked with me on Thirteenth Street.

There was an amber lightbulb in the bedroom and there was an amber glow over everything. And two tall Jamaican poets standing over me, then picking me from the bed. I'd lost weight because I was afraid to go out for food. And when I did, I bought two of everything so it looked like I wasn't alone, in case a rapist was stalking me. I lived on coffee, one black, one regular, and cheese Danishes for a month.

I remember them holding my face over a sink, trying to make me throw up. Then holding my head out the window. And cold night air. And police banging on the apartment door. Someone had reported black men climbing a fire escape. The police asked me if everything was OK. I stood in front of them, in my white housecoat, shaking from the effects of attempted suicide, the taste of vomit in my mouth, and my eyes not really clear.

"Everything...is fine," I said.

I looked at those policemen in dark blue, as if they were in one movie and I were in a completely separate one. And mine was in black and white. And amber.

The risk of sexual attack is doubled for women who have lived through childhood sexual abuse. People live through. Just as a country can be the site of a battle, so can a body be the scene of a crime.

Flying to Newfoundland a few weeks later for Christmas was a mistake. My mother couldn't handle rape, suicide attempts, my mind, or me. Standing by a radiator in the downstairs hallway before I'd even removed my coat, she said in that tone people use when a reply isn't wanted, "You're not going to ruin anyone's Christmas here," cleared her throat, lit a cigarette, and walked away to the rest of the family in the kitchen. It was clear. I was to be silent. About everything. To everyone.

She took me to Bingo games instead. "B-6...G-54." No one's routine was interrupted. A week later, I flew back to Manhattan. Cheap hotel room. Pigeons on a windowsill. A daily account in some newspapers of how many had been killed on each side in Vietnam. Like a hockey score. Or the Olympics.

If evil is not destroyable, then the saving grace is that neither is love.

There is an amber glow over the meadow, as if a lamp has been left on. I want to touch it, to see if it feels like velvet. I listen to the music of Ferron. But I want to listen to the sky instead. Tears roll from my eyes to my neck, resting there, like pearls. Wind is blowing memories away like sand in a Tibetan Mandela. This is matins. The great prayer of the night. This is a hidden church, the most spectacular cathedral ever built, except now I've found it. This is something created for royalty, and I am sitting on a wooden bench right in the middle of it, wearing a double layer of flannel shirts.

I leave the meadow, walk back up the hill, punch the secret code into the main door, enter the dark hallway, walk to my room, and change into my nightgown for a second time. I need to pace. Am I returning to New York or not? I walk down to the main chapel in my nightgown. Tiptoeing in bare feet. The red vigil light sends a dancing shadow on the ceiling. The only light except for the dim hallway light outside. There is peace in this wooden chapel—in this complex.

I pace the long, dark hallways in my nightgown. Am I staying to learn whatever it is I feel I am to learn? Will this moment come around again?

If this retreat house really is in alignment with a ley line, I am beginning to feel as if the core of the energy exists in the meadow itself. But whether it is or isn't, there is some form of energy in the meadow.

Everyone in this building is asleep except me. Every woman in this building knows what she is doing in the morning. Except me. The hallways are silent. It is almost 3 A.M. and I have to be up in three hours. I return to my room and go to sleep because I have to get up.

In Ireland, there were the famous "fairy passes," invisible straight paths, that ran from one rath (Prehistoric earthwork) to another.

— Paul Devereux, *The Long Trip*

In China, evil spirits were thought to travel in straight lines, so the [funeral] route had to be blocked with a wall containing a charm.

— Danny Sullivan, *Ley Lines: A Comprehensive Guide to Alignments*

MONDAY, 6 A.M.

I'm awake and not tired. There is almost no sound, only stillness and light.

After meditation in the meadow I have toast with butter and jam, and cantaloupe. There's meat but I don't eat it.

My friend arrives in her car. We've agreed over the phone that she will support my decision, whatever it might be.

I decide not to return to New York. To face the unknown, alone, with nuns in the woods. To stay for the remainder of the week. To learn to think about the past. About the fragility of the earth. About the future, and hope. About creativity. My own. Which didn't arrive in a neatly wrapped package. My creativity arrived in a crate with bars bending and breaking with wildness, a wild hairy creature wanting to be free. I decide to stay to do archeology work. To practise dowsing. To search for myself, using a meadow as a sacred rod. To listen. To drink tea in solitude, and breathe in the crispness of cool air.

We're required to look back. Not to stay there. But to look back.

I've arrived for only a weekend and now don't have supplies. Sister Theresa drives me into town. Batteries, toothpaste, and a newspaper, which I don't read. We visit a shrine, and walk amid statues, trees, and a grotto with a black stone from Lourdes, France, site of Bernadette's visions. Hecate, goddess of the crossroads, of the dark side, had tiny clusters of stones placed in her honour in European villages. I feel as if I'm at a crossroads. And I pray to Mary, Hecate, Bernadette, for myself and for the nun with a car.

We return to the complex. The temperature drops at night and my socks won't dry on a contraption I've designed with safety pins and a hanger. Another woman gives me two pairs. Sister Norma. And they are my old school colours, blue and gold. I am now wearing the clothes of a nun. The character begins with the foot.

We used to wear ribbons to hockey games in Newfoundland. The Catholics against the Publics. Their colours were red and grey and they always seemed more powerful. Maybe it was the red, the Jesus colour. The ribbons attached with pins and fluttered as we stomped our feet on wooden bleachers. Standing, because it was too cold to sit. Gloved hands around cups of steaming hot chocolate. Voices screaming the length of a hockey rink.

The group seems happy that I've stayed. I have no idea what I'm doing but I'm happy.

In the main building, before lunch, a sister asks if I'd like to help her set up a chapel, and we trim wildflowers over an old sink in a storage room.

Flowers. Silk. Real. Wild. The garden variety. A single rose wrapped in cellophane and received as a gift. A dried bouquet left over from an episode of *All My Children*. Fabric roses from a costume at the Met. Flowers in sidewalk gardens and on windowsills. Tissue paper roses. The Shakespeare Garden in Central Park. Flowers in the fake snow of Christmas displays, poinsettias living in Styrofoam. Dried flowers in every book I've ever owned. The War of the Roses. Queen Anne's lace. The morning glories Sister Mary Gertrude drew on the 1950s blackboard, delicate blue petals growing in front of an overcrowded silent classroom, chalk leaves inching their way towards the window. These flowers too, needed light. Roots never existing. These flowers were always without foundation and simply floated across the room.

Flowers on altars. At birth and death. Pens with flowers on top, plastic petals scribbling across a page. The last elegant white rose for a friend dying from AIDS. Bouquets of Canadian wildflowers. A circle of delicate pink roses held together by one thin thread, a birthday gift from a friend.

The endless, endless flowers.

We select vases from a high shelf and I am given the gold box containing the Eucharist, the very symbol of Jesus himself. Standing by the elevator I realize I don't have enough information. So, holding Jesus with one hand and the elevator button with the other, I yell down the hall, "Are we going up or down?"

The answer is "up," as she walks towards me carrying wild irises and a lace cloth. I should have known.

We place the cloth on a low table with the gold box in the centre, arrange flowers, and fluff cushions on the floor. We've created a chapel. And it's three doors from The Queen of Peace Room.

During the afternoon, one of the women tells me that the Pope had forbidden all dialogue regarding women's ordination. All discussion is officially forbidden. I say I find this insulting. So does she. I say women should build their own churches. After getting the Pope's name correct, I draft a letter challenging the Vatican. "To His Holiness Pope John II, Hildegard wrote to her Pope and today I am writing to mine....Those who are silencing this dialogue are not acting with wisdom. With all due respect, Dear Holy Father, a lot has happened since Christ chose the first twelve apostles." (Months later, a monsignor responds on behalf of the Vatican, informing me that the Pope is praying for me.)

We talk about our different work. Shelters for battered women. Intensive care units of hospitals. Instructors of children. Council for the helpless. These women work in schools and prisons and hospitals. Each works until her head hits the pillow. I work backstage at opera houses and television studios. Talk with famous people about costumes and personal things. Kathleen Battle, Macy's Day Parade, Carnegie Hall, *Law and Order*, *All My Children*. I work until my head hits the pillow. We talk about the snow angels we made as children. About the bodies of little girls dumped on the side roads of Bangladesh, their organs removed for sale. Only girl bodies are found. Boy children are allowed to live, they have value. We talk about water. When the water is gone, we're all gone. Nothing survives without water.

I want one of those whistles that teachers had long ago. When things got out of hand, they blew a long, loud piercing sound and all noise stopped. I need to think and I need a big whistle. I'm seeing the world through the eyes of women who work with the crippled and homeless and starving, who shelter the battered and broken. They are the new apostles and are in touch with the suffering.

We discuss everything in the afternoon on the porch, taking only short breaks for coffee and cookies or the very tiny muffins.

We discuss dreams and visions, starvation and greed, AIDS and stigmas, breast cancer and the woman in the group battling that illness. We discuss walls and tearing some of them down.

We're like one large herd of wild deer, looking out over the fringes of a meadow, talking about the environment, the planet, and its people. Talking about soup, human rights, and Africa.

In an afternoon of marathon conversation we discuss almost everything. Except epilepsy. That word is so boarded shut in my mind, not even the meadow can dislodge it.

What caused my seizures? What's preventing them now? Which cell allows the brain to be calm in one person but not in another? If it's true that our bodies remember the past, maybe activity in the brain, in relationship to seizures, can be triggered by old knowledge, by traumatic memories crammed within and looking for a place to discharge. The brain, in photographs, sometimes looks a little like an exploding nuclear bomb.

Without warning, a body can find itself relocated to another part of the universe, memory erased. Seconds before it had been walking upright. Before there might have been a lightness in the voice, a lilt. Then without warning the body is frozen, trapped inside a world of then and now. Two selves. The one who fell and one who didn't. Both living in fear. One afraid of the seizure. One afraid of the stigma. This is how epilepsy feels sometimes. To me.

What was the triggering neuron causing the blackout, the momentary explosion? The body makes notes. Avoid this, stay away from that, don't ever go there again. Like a map through a dangerous forest—if you go down that road again you may be attacked. Self promises to be vigilant, to watch for stressful situations like a deer watches for danger.

Severe stress can do to a person with epilepsy, what smoke can do to a person with lung cancer. The brain becomes unable to breathe. Memories of unspeakable experiences stick to the body like sweat on a hot day. They remain, like a scar. But severe stress makes only some people apprehensive. The brain, like a shoulder or calf muscle, has a predisposition to weakness in some people but not in others. We don't know why, we just know.

Every muscle moved has an anatomy. Each muscle has a memory and it holds onto its past like a prison guard with bloated key rings. Moments from the past once filled with terror, linger. Depression, exhaustion, stress, incest, food deprivation, abandonment, and severe headaches can all cause seizures.

Paralyzed, the mind travels elsewhere, anywhere, blankness. The brain has learned disappearing skills. Living with seizures is living life on the edge most of the time. The body owning the brain has been attacked. The brain has been attacked. Signals criss-cross and brain waves tangle like shoelaces on a windy clothesline. They collide with clothespins and workshirts and things made from lace. The brain is a clothesline, and seizures make messages tangle. Epilepsy is something like that.

Living with seizures is living life with the incomprehensible—an unseen fist can reach from the sky and push the body to the ground. Something happens. Stress triggers a cell, a neuron, and the electrical system in the brain instantly rewires itself. The interruption can be so brief, even the body owning the brain is unaware of it. Sensitive EEG machines might capture something. Epilepsy can be blank stares in moments of fear, but it can also be broken bones or a disfigured face found at an intersection, unconscious and bleeding, parts that were once on the left, now on the right. A medical worker shouting, "She had a seizure! She had a seizure!" as if someone were about to win an award. Experts are called and the face reassembled; the body owning the face tries to vanish. To melt. Who did this? The self who became dizzy and fell, or the self struck by a speeding car? The self whose neurons flew in all directions? There are few answers for the self with epilepsy.

Stress happens. Seizures happen. Cars run wild on busy streets. And at moments of life-threatening stress, the brain forfeits all memory. It uses all of its power to simply keep breathing. Memory isn't paramount. Breathing is.

The body gathers new memories. Gardens in springtime, lilacs leaning on fences, tulip and ivy competing for space. Erase from the mind whatever happened yesterday. The self seeks knowledge and calm in a world that is upright. A world without violence. A world without stigma.

Epilepsy is clothed in social stigma and so much inaccurate, outdated information. The most important things have yet to be written. There is no known cause and no known cure. It's a little like AIDS, just not as publicly recognized.

If a person with epilepsy were to wear a little ribbon, it would probably depict a clothesline, shoelaces going in all directions, and the words "When we get back on our feet, someone is going to have hell to pay."

The layers to the handicap I once had to conceal are thick with intensity. Like large pieces of Greek pastry. Giant slabs of baklava. Pistachio nuts going in all directions. They're like an explosion, an eruption; like the Fourth of July, except no one applauds.

Later, walking in the silence of the woods in my bare feet, the wind kisses my face and I sigh out loud. I don't mean to, but I do. I apologize into the air for disturbing the quiet. Monumental obstructions are beginning to melt. I read everything in sight. "I don't want to repeat the past. I don't want to repeat the past." I keep repeating this until I realize what I'm doing. There are bones that need tending. A person in need of healing. For years I have abandoned her. Others have abandoned her and I've been taking my cue from them. I need wisdom and power and strength. Things I've been denied.

In the evening I sit on the steps outside the chapel, watching the evening sky change colour while I put finishing touches on a second letter to the Pope.

"Are you really a lesbian?" one of the sisters asks.

No one had ever asked me that. The issue had been mentioned earlier in the week when I'd read a poem about loving women. I played a lesbian in a movie once, years ago, but they have no way of knowing this. Her question is followed by silence. Both hers and mine. I know I prefer the company of gentle people. Gentle women. But I've never been questioned by a nun on a porch outside a church door about sexuality. Honesty seemed imperative.

"Well," I stumble, "I prefer the company of women. I seem to get my greatest strength from women. I definitely don't want big gymnastic acts of sex but I prefer being with women. So, I guess if that makes me a lesbian, I'm a lesbian."

She smiles and steps out of the red sports car she's parked in front of the church.

"Good," she says. "Let's go to the meeting. They're waiting for us."

We walk together, across the grey stone path, beneath birch and maple, cross over by the marble outdoor statue of Mary, half hidden behind a spruce tree and walk up the clean wooden steps together, to take notes and talk about the magic and sacredness of the earth.

These women listen to me like I've never been listened to before. They don't say an ungentle word. They give me warm socks, drives into town, and walk with me after meals. Some of them belong to the same order as the nuns who beat me. If we wait long enough, does the past correct itself?

We share mystic stories. I tell them about an old vision. A full moon surrounded by a double ring of fiery crimson light. Everything shifting slightly. Then clouds and the fiery rings again. Then the figure of a tall dark-haired man in white flowing robes, floating from the midst of this cloud formation. He sails upwards out of the circle and into the blue blackness of the sky, like an angel or Christ. The vision didn't scare me. Being unable to talk to anyone about it, until now, scared me more.

What do cloistered people do with their thoughts? They don't stop thinking.

We read the words of Chief Seattle, Celtic saints, Gandhi, and Mary Oliver. I read my own prayers. Songs about the environment written for a Canadian composer.

I feel as if I am starting something over again. In a very profound way. And the notes have grown:

- Notice your fear.
- Have patience with everyone, especially and most importantly with oneself.
- Walk with lightning, walk with thunder, and walk with the heaviest of heavy rainstorms.
- Listen to the times around the pain, the times that preceded it, and the times that follow it.
- Ask why you're here, it doesn't matter if you don't know, it only matters that you ask yourself the question.
- If we are all part of the same world—what is this meaning now in the face of war and famine.
- Learn to recognize your limitations, if you have any.
- Let some things be.
- No amount of sadness will change things.
- Some jobs are good to be fired from.
- Imagination—don't lose it.
- Make choices, choose those things which fill your soul with joy, that let you breathe freely.

Later, after dinner, after the last conversation of the evening, and after walking alone on the paths surrounding the complex, I walk down to the meadow again, and into it. As if it were a river. The lights are there again. Long wide bands of gold and pink and amber stretching across the night sky. And the countless numbers of brilliant stars are there. Beauty is coming from all directions. Everything about this complex is magic and unpredictable. Without borders, without an equal. Like a small café in New York in the 1960s. Like the wide night sky in front of me.

The Caffe Cino began before it actually began. It began part way down the street. Outdoor golden, amber, and rose lights, not neon, spilled across the sidewalk and made their way towards you, silently, like dancers, as you approached. Everything about the Caffe Cino began before it began. Inside the room, like the mystery of ley lines, all time stopped. There was no time inside except magic time.

History claims that Anne Boleyn had a slight defect in one of her fingernails. Many of us who were a part of the Caffe had slight defects. A broken heart, a broken past, a broken family. It's no coincidence that we came together in the middle of a war. Protest marches, civil rights, draft-card burning, bra burning, communal living, and long hair. Puppet theatre, free stores, body paint, denim clothes, drug overdoses. Political poetry, tie-dye, and thousands of men who looked like Jesus. Everything happening simultaneously. The evening news showing a series of bloody body bags being carried across the screen. Sitar music, daisies, semi-nude cello players, and Be-Ins, folk-singing in Washington Square Park until it was banned, the 60s were a time of love and constant war news, of perpetual contradiction. People had liquid codeine in one hand and brown rice in the other.[1] Rice farmers in Cambodia stood rather than hide as bombs riddled the earth around them; by standing, less of their body was on the ground and vulnerable. Writers, actors, construction workers, ballerinas, and lawyers, all came together as if we'd received a calling. Like alchemists huddled over a script. The Caffe touched every part of my body. Every bone, muscle, membrane. Every part of my being was changed. My memory explodes when I think of it. Joe Cino, a Sicilian, arrived in Manhattan from Buffalo, on February 7th, 1948, dur-

---

1 In a ten-year undeclared war, America sent half a million soldiers into Vietnam and bombarded the country with three times the tonnage of bombs dropped on Germany and Japan in World War II. Helen Caldicott, *Missile Envy* (New York: Bantam Books, 1986), 215.

ing a blizzard, by bus, sixteen and broke. He worked two jobs, saved money, and opened the Caffe on a Friday in December 1958. I left Newfoundland in 1962. Those facts are recorded.

But how Off-Off-Broadway became a reality isn't. One day it was suddenly there. At 31 Cornelia Street. It began as a little café with poetry readings. A few years later, plays by gay writers, feminist and political writers. The Caffe was Joe's gift to the world. He invented the Grimm's brothers, not the other way around. It was a mountain of fantasy rising out of thin air in Greenwich Village in the 60s. Acting, clearing tables, and directing were synonymous. People worked together like parts of the sky. Joe was always the moon. At different times we were stars, clouds, the landscape surrounding everything, an unexplained planet, and rain. But Joe remained the moon, this never changed. Pushing boundaries, defying limits, equally at home with cowboys and angels, crossing lines that said *don't cross.*

Johnny Dodd's genius lighting could light a cup but not its saucer. Lights were dimmed, stage lights would appear on an area eight feet square and the room would open, like a chakra. Performances were done with or without an audience. They were done for the walls, for the room.

My first job was stage-managing for Tom Eyen, with an actress who was to become the blueprint for a character Tom later created for Bette Midler. And I stage-managed Bette a year later.

The Caffe was in three parts: the door with its outside metal gate; the narrow room with its walls and stage and mismatched ice cream parlour furniture; and the tiny kitchen. An evening breeze drifted through the open door. The ceiling was a maze of intricate lighting equipment, fluttering stars, and wind chimes from Chinatown. The walls were a series of giant collages, pictures of saints, and twinkle lights, Marilyn Monroe and Allen Ginsberg. Jesus and the Statue of Liberty, Greta Garbo, James Dean, glossy eight-by-tens, homemade cards with glitter, autographed pictures of divas, Bette Midler's tiny resume—an address, a phone number, where she'd graduated from high school, and three summer stock plays; the bakery and cheese-shop phone numbers, more stars. Belly dancing and Christmas carols at midnight, in August. Mozart, *The Barber of Seville*, Gene Autry, Kate Smith, Shirley Temple, Billie Holiday, and Maria Callas all overlapped. The smell of cappuccino and pastry. The

Birthday Book with everyone's name. I felt as if I'd been beamed into the Caffe from another planet.

On Sunday nights, the smell of cinnamon blended with the smell of Spic 'n Span from Slippery, the man who mopped the floor. I don't know which came first, his name, or the state of the floor. Behind the espresso machine, narrow shelves lined with cups. Tiny cans of expensive tuna. Kenny Burgess, the artist, making sandwiches. He and Joe, two Scorpios in the kitchen. Joe even knew how to make scrambled eggs using a little steam attachment on the machine. A surrealistic curtain of bells, tangled with ribbons and roses, stretched across in front of the espresso machine, a musical explosion by Joe when someone gave an especially good performance.

To the right of the espresso machine, a patterned urn filled with Cino matchbooks designed by Joe's lover, and the Caffe phone number CH3-9753. Below it, a large carton of coins, mostly pennies, for emergencies.

Joe gave me the phone payment once, in rolled coins piled high on a table. The phone man arrived, just the two of us in the room, and I explained that the payment was all there. As I stood with the irritated man, watching him try to figure out how he was going to deal with this mountain of currency, an extension phone, hooked up illegally, started to ring.

"Where's that phone?" he asked.

"What phone?" I said.

"That phone," he said, "The one ringing."

"I don't hear any phone," I said.

He walked towards the sound and discovered the illegal instrument. But we always had a phone, sometimes three. If you helped Joe with the room, you were a Rockette. There was nothing higher than a Rockette. *Phonaca*, that was his word for phony. Joe's eyes were large, brown, and filled with passion. He could hold you with his eyes. He became my measuring stick for the word *family* for the rest of my life.

He had a secret language. It centred on the word *Ella*. "Pass the Ella." "Here comes Ella." In time it was understandable but it took time. "Put the Ella on Ella's table, and bring the other Ella back!"

There were no rules. There were three rules. It was simultaneous. None and three. The rules were—do what you have to do, do it for the room, it's magic time.

I walked into the Caffe late one afternoon and was asked, as if *no* were not an option, "Can you build a waterfall?"

"Sure," I said, and put down my manuscript of poetry. Allen Ginsberg said I wrote like Wallace Stevens or William Carlos Williams. I can't remember which. I found out what there was to build it with (sequins), where it was to fall (in the centre of the stage), who it was to fall upon (Ondine, from Warhol's factory, and Charles Stanley), when it was needed (tonight). I clustered sequins inside cardboard, with a string that ran across the ceiling. When the string was pulled, the cardboard tipped, and sequins rained down. Aquamarine sequins. We thought of everything in the 60s. Magic.

Magic is why people stayed and worked for a sandwich. Some-times enough for subway tokens. Subways were cheap, five cents before 1950. It wasn't until 1966 that they'd gone up to twenty cents. It had nothing to do with money and everything to do with freedom and creativity and working so hard you thought you'd collapse and never get up again. It was about more. The word. Wild elegant creativity, and freedom to create. The human skin has the same membranes as the ear, what had we been hearing before and what were we hearing now? Another sound had been introduced, another touch. Another way of learning about the world.

Andy Warhol came in at midnight with an entourage. He wanted the rights to my picture. A poster on the Caffe wall but the photographer refused. Bernadette Peters, Bette Midler, Harvey Keitel began there. Lanford Wilson, Tom Eyen, Sam Shepard, Robert Patrick, Paul Foster, and every new playwright paving the way for the next century had roots there. The underground playwright H.M. Harry Koutoukas was so important, the Caffe probably wouldn't have survived without him. Candy Darling rehearsed there. Everyone rehearsed there.

One day the person hiring impostors for the television show, *To Tell The Truth* came into the Caffe, and hired me as an impostor for the world champion figure skater, Petra Burka.

I didn't have a television set and watched the show from a revolving stool in a corner luncheonette. The stranger next to me looked at the screen, then at me.

"Is that you up there?" he asked.

"Yes" I said.

And the two of us watched me on national television lying to the entire world about who I really was. I received three out of four votes, one hundred and fifty dollars, and returned to the Caffe and whatever thirty-minute play was being done that week. The plays had to be about thirty minutes. The chairs were so uncomfortable no one could sit much longer.

The Caffe overlapped with everything. Like the nuns in Newfoundland, only opposite. Peter, Paul, and Mary, the Beatles, Andy Warhol, and Valerie Solanas.

I can't remember how I met Valerie. She was like the Caffe. One day she was suddenly there. Valerie and I slept together on two occasions. At her room in the Chelsea Hotel. Valerie was the only woman I slept with in the 60s. We never called it forbidden love. We just called it sleeping together. And we did. In each other's arms like two old tired women.

"Someone should write a play about you," she once said, "And call it Cleopatra." I think if people had tried to harm me while I was with Valerie, she would have killed them with her bare hands.

Joe Cino and Valerie Solanas were alike in some ways. People saw what they needed. A Rorschach test.

One morning Joe called me at home.

"They're doing the umbrellas for *Dames at Sea*," he said, "and I won't let anyone touch them until you get here. Come in now," he emphasized and hung up.

I took the subway that day, not knowing for sure what "umbrellas" meant. It could have been like "Ella." It could have been anything. *Dames at Sea* was a thirty-minute musical created on an eight-foot stage with a very young Bernadette Peters. I spent hours gluing silver sequins to clear, opened plastic umbrellas in the tiny dressing room. Open umbrellas were forbidden in the room, but plastic bubbles with magic raindrops were allowed. For "Raining In My Heart," Bernadette's signature song. Thousands of umbrellas in other productions, in other countries over the years, have all had sequins glued to plastic. This is how it originated.

Dames At Sea was a take-off on everything pure and innocent. It played to over-packed houses for two months. The room was officially full when two people were seated on top of the cigarette machine. It was the longest run in Cino history. Everyone passed the basket. Financial success for an entire summer. Eight weeks later, a producer moved it to a large theatre, Carol Burnett saw it; invited Bernadette onto her show and the rest is history. I think Joe would have let *Dames* run for fifty years if he'd been given a choice.

In 1967 Joe's lover was accidentally electrocuted in a freak accident. The harassment from New York City Government was unrelenting. They denied Joe a licence to operate and they unmercifully harassed him because he didn't have one. It wasn't a bar, Joe never served liquor. It was a café without a category. It was an illegal opera that took ten years to reach its final climatic note.

In March I covered Cino matches with glitter for St. Patrick's Day. I asked Joe to reach the jar I'd hidden on a shelf. While reaching he asked what I was doing.

"You've covered the sacred name!" he screamed. "No more surprises!" and he threw the matches across the room. He was devastated with grief over his lover's death and I'd stupidly covered the design. My mind flashed to memories of violence. I walked to the bathroom and stood there, silently. The bathroom that day was gold: ceiling, walls, fixtures, floor, and mirror frame. When I walked back to the room a cup of coffee was resting on my manuscript. A gift from Joe. I hadn't anticipated a gift and didn't acknowledge it. I walked towards the door, heavy, like I'd become five times my weight. I remember a voice saying, "Is she leaving?" and there was silence as I walked away.

Drugs were in the room and people who sold them. Warhol was in the room late at night with the factory phone number, AT9-1298. In March of 1967, Joe tried to cut the pain from his heart. His desperate loneliness. The pain of his dead lover. Financial problems. The operas going on inside his own mind. Alone in the room, he slashed at his body as if it were the enemy. Hara-kiri. St. Vincent's Hospital received more blood than at any other time since World War II.

All the drinks at the Caffe were cold. No one knew how to work the espresso machine.

I wish *The Madness of Lady Bright* hadn't been the last play Joe got to see, not because it was bad, but because it was so despairingly sad, the story of an aging gay man, desperately lonely and with absolutely no hope. I wish I hadn't glittered those goddamn matches. I blame drugs for the death of Joe Cino. I blame a lot of things.

Joe Cino was pronounced dead on Sunday evening, 2 April, 1967. People streamed in and out of the Caffe for hours. It was as if each of us were experiencing the final breath. The slowing down of the organs, what remained, the slowing of the heart and lungs, blood cooling, hair resting, limp. Fingernails stopping their growth, the beard stopping its push outward. Each hair slowing down. It was a night of death. The death of Joe Cino and the heart of Off-Off Broadway. Different for each of us and the collective pain was unrelenting. I remember dimness. Sounds of boots on a wooden floor. A man with his face in another man's hands. Both of them weeping by the espresso machine. Like a tableaux from the Crucifixion. Joe didn't commit suicide. He loved life. A man, out of control with a massive dose of drugs, supplied to him, committed suicide. Joe Cino was murdered: by something. That's my theory.

On April 10th at Judson Church, the memorial program cover was wordless. A black and white photo of Joe, wearing an apron I'd made for him from leftover *Dames at Sea* stars. White stars on a red apron. Inside the church, the dancer Eddie Barthonn, his naked body covered completely in gold glitter, walked on his hands, through the entire church, up and down the aisles. Bernadette Peters sang "Raining in My Heart." Johnny Dodd made blue spotlights appear to weep on an empty stage as the voice of Kate Smith pierced the silence. "When the Moon Comes over the Mountain."

Joe had been our foundation, our home, room, walls, ceiling, and roof.

Six of us grouped together and tried to keep the Caffe operating. In August, the dancer and writer Charles Stanley, who'd become the strength behind everyone, came flying out the Caffe door as I slowly walked up Cornelia, said the night's production had cancelled, that we were doing the comic book *Snow White* instead and I was in it. If a show rarely cancelled at the Caffe, we improvised with high comic-book drama. I asked him what part he wanted me to play as we ran, and held onto his hand as he took long strides. "Snow White," he said, as we ran through the middle of the street.

My entire life flashed before my eyes, past, present, and future. This was like *Live from the Met*, except it was Live from the Cino. I felt as if I'd gone into orbit. "I found her," he said, as we ran, still holding hands through a packed Caffe.

In the tiny dressing room the playwright H.M. Harry Koutoukas was in costume and make-up as the evil stepmother. Kenny Burgess, as all the forest creatures, was a walking collage of fur pieces, feathers, twinkle lights, and pictures from *National Geographic*. The playwright Robert Patrick was ready as Doc and the entire haunted forest with large plastic ferns from Lamston's and indescribable determination. The playwright David Starkweather was Sneezy. People were ready as Grumpy and Dopey. The Prince was handsome. The Royal Huntsman had just returned from Fire Island, was suffering a heavy sunburn, and could wear only the top half of the costume. Charles was the Magic Mirror and did everything else as well, lights, sound, direction. All this had been put into place in a matter of hours. Minutes.

I entered the comic book as one would enter a building. In the fleeing-through-the-forest scene on the tiny wooden stage, Robert Patrick, hiding behind a piece of white curtain, waved plastic ferns in my face with complete and utter franticness, as if he himself were being chased by demons. Charles created a lightning storm that fell over the entire room, accompanied by a blaring aria, and I raced from one end of the eight-foot stage to the other, back and forth and back and forth, and back and forth, until I collapsed, exhausted, to the floor, fourteen times a week, for two weeks. And every night, Kenny, as the forest creatures, knelt beside me as I moved silently and slowly, with my right hand, imaginary branches, so we could see the imaginary house in the imaginary clearing. I was never taught how to do this. I knew it instinctively. I'd learned it up the highway. And the memory remained to be retrieved in this room. Every performance, the dwarfs were different and the number was always changing. Over two hundred people were dwarfs. Snow White's wedding dress was a priest's white chasuble. In the death-to-the-evil-stepmother scene, the dwarfs threw Italian pastries at Harry, grabbing them from the silver tray and firing cannolis, rum fluffs, and napoleons as if they were grenades. I have no idea if this was planned or impromptu. But H.M. Koutoukas, the evil stepmother of Snow White, swooned under a mountain of whipped cream and pastry.

Charles Stanley was one of the most gracious, gifted, and talented people I have ever known. Of the hundreds and hundreds of people who worked at the Caffe, few became as famous as Bette Midler and Bernadette Peters. Lanford Wilson received the Pulitzer Prize years later but he was a dwarf in 1967. Harvey Keitel became famous in Hollywood but was probably a dwarf in the 60s. In *Snow*

White, everyone was a dwarf. From Pulitzer Prize winners to strangers who were walking down Cornelia Street and were free for an hour if a dwarf was needed.

The only one missing was Joe.

Winter was like confetti thrown into the blades of a full volume fan, emotions going in all directions. People found the memory of Joe too painful. Valerie kept phoning the Caffe wanting Charles to produce her play. Charles referred to her as "your friend." She was afraid Warhol was going to steal her idea. There were no Xerox machines in the 60s and she'd trusted him with the only copy of her manuscript. She was having trouble at her hotel and wanted to stay with me at my hotel room. I said a difficult no. I didn't know how to cope with anyone anymore, including myself. In 1968 I received the Langston Hughes Award for poetry.

In March the Caffe closed for good. We surrendered to exhaustion and New York City politics. The room never, ever looked so sad. The Caffe closed on March 17, 1968, Saint Patrick's Day. An era had ended. People took parts of the room with them. No one wanted to leave it abandoned and alone on the street. Pictures were ripped from the walls and put into boxes and brought to Lincoln Center Library, where they remain, some with icing remnants from the battle scene in Snow White. People took crystals, dishes, posters, everything was suddenly a relic. I took the gold mirror, a teapot, and a blue cup. Someone took the entire little stage.

In June, Valerie shot Andy Warhol. She'd taken her fear and rage too far. *Hair* opened on Broadway. There was a statewide moon vigil in Central Park followed by a major Vietnam protest march.

The 1960s were like the wild west. Anyone who denies it simply wasn't there. One New Year's Eve, a friend of a friend, a junkie, phoned the time operator at least a dozen times—with a needle hanging from his vein. He wanted to pull off at exactly New Year's, on the exact second. To bring in the year with a pure heroin high. We watched and waited with him. At midnight, exactly, he did it. And everyone was relieved when it was over. No one laughed. Or cheered.

Half a million people with flowers in their hair chanted peace in a field in upstate New York. A man walked on the moon. John F. Kennedy, Martin Luther King, Malcolm X, Robert Kennedy were all assassinated. The 60s ended with unmitigated violence.

The Caffe Cino shaped who I am. That tiny room at 31 Cornelia Street gave me my sense of the world.

The nuns at this complex are like people from the Caffe in some ways. No judgments. Only companionship, acceptance, coffee with tiny muffins, and a touch of kindness.

Every touch placed on the skin penetrates; this is why hand lotion works. Or a nicotine patch. Every touch penetrates to the cells where memories have lived for decades. We are powerless over this. Memories linger and the cells drench with yesterday, until memories become simply one more part of the anatomy demanding attention. Logic and math aren't involved.

On the way back up the hill to the complex, wind shakes trees near the outdoor statue of Mary, making blue shadows fall across her face. It shakes windows and makes long-necked street lamps sway like tall stalks of wheat. Stars are bursting through the dark night sky. The wind pushes me gently against hedges that are trimmed too closely. It makes doors slam and moves objects that are attempting to deny it. It makes wishing sounds. It is a wind of change. Of cleansing. Like a good cry. Like those tears that fall when we realize, late at night, alone, on any ordinary evening, what an extraordinary point we have just reached in our lives. We cry sometimes for days. For weeks. We think our hearts will break. We may ask ourselves, will I ever stop crying? Will these tears ever end? And the answer is no. Only the reason will change. We will cry with our eyes wide open, while looking at a starry sky. While walking amid the solitude of trees. As we move, one foot after the other, through a thick, soft snow, but we'll never stop crying. Only the reason will change.

I walk the pathways and look into a sky bursting with stars. Clouds racing across the moon. Look for a vision the way native people do. Look behind hedges, through shifting leaf patterns. Hear beads I can't see click and clink with the wind. Hear the swish of a gown on a staircase, though there are no stairs. I want to reach out. See if my hand can touch an invisible sleeve. But I choose not to. I choose to let the space itself become a presence. And I realize I'll never be alone again. Unless I want to be.

I walk past the barns and meeting house, enter the secret code and return to my room. I listen to the soft sounds of women saying goodnight, doors opening and closing gently, and footsteps returning from the chapel.

I adjust the electric travel clock and prepare for tomorrow. I have some control over the clock.

If this complex is really in alignment with a ley line, I want to know two things—is this why I am recalling so many memories? And if there is an alignment, is the ley in alignment with the past? With anybody's past?

Just as the human body incorpo-
rates channels along which life
energy and blood flow, so it is
believed that the earth contains
similar channels called "the
veins of the dragon," in feng
shui literature. The wide
variations in the topogra-
phy of the earth determine
favorable and unfavorable
sites, or auspicious and
inauspicious sites.
— Henry B. Lin, *The Art and
Science of Feng Shui*

Feng Shui contends that the
environment is crowded with
powerful, but invisible energy
lines.
— Lillian Too, *The Fundamentals
of Feng Shui*

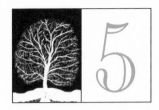

TUESDAY, DAWN

The light wakes me, or maybe it's the stillness. Everything is at a junction. Night sounds are making room for day sounds and there's a space in between. Maybe the space woke me. The wide spacious maple outside the Queen of Peace window is silent. One leaf flutters a tiny wave of green. A bird gives one whistle—as if it's a signal. The new day can begin.

Morning sounds fill the hallway. Slow footsteps, muffled voices, sleepy "Good Mornings," running water. Everyone is preparing for the meadow, morning, and breakfast.

I raise the window all the way and a warm breeze fills the room. The bouquet of wildflowers from yesterday has wilted already. Wildflowers don't survive long in captivity.

I look at the magnificent tree and realize that I haven't really seen it before. Not each branch, the bark, the trunk, birds resting on it, clouds passing above it, the way it fits into the ground, the way it reaches its arms into sky—touching space. The way it's ringed below with flowers and vines and small white stones. The way sunlight pours through branches, then falls against the sides of the barn, as if the light and shadows themselves are paint.

Everyone meets in the meadow and sits in the light of sunrise. A poem is read, then quiet again and the sounds of birds and crickets, wind through trees, smells of earth, dew on grass, wild-blooming flowers. A tiny bell rings somewhere. A gentle velvet sound. Birds rush back and forth in a morning feeding frenzy.

Women slowly walk up the hill to the main house for breakfast. A tray with pancakes and fruit. A glass bowl with blueberries.

The food we eat and the way we eat is a direct link to our past. There are no barriers separating the brain from the stomach. No little corners for the mind to hide in. We become aware of the reality by experiencing the change.

After breakfast we speak for an hour, about finding our path, our goal, about how much easier things can be when we have a semblance of destination. Nothing else is scheduled for the morning. A few of the women drive into town. Two read in their rooms. I keep gravitating to the meadow, as if there is something there for me to learn, as if it were leading somewhere. So my goal is to follow the meadow.

After lunch we talk about remembering. Uncovering and discovering.

We talk about the past. Just what I don't want to do. The past cuts through me like slices of lightning.

I need a great deal of space and begin by talking about the wind, the wilder it is the more focused I become. As if internal cobwebs are being removed. I let wind wash over me like a river. I welcome it. I remember cold winds. Being cold can make you desperate. Can make you reach for things you never thought you'd reach for. Hold onto people you never should be near. You run to the arms of danger because danger is standing there wanting to hold you and this is all you've wanted. To be held. Desperate and cold, you welcome the arms of a minefield. You gamble with your own life. You enter the minefield desperate, and continue to walk, even though something blows away a part of your body. What would be the logic in turning around now? You're in the middle of a minefield. All directions are the same.

When we are children we are innocent. But when we are adults we allow ourselves to be betrayed. And if we have an abusive history we accept things. Signs are ignored. They can't be read anyway. And they keep changing. Loss of self-esteem and the humiliation and shame accompanying it can cripple as severely as any automobile accident; can break the spirit as easily as if it were simply a shattered bone. Incest, rape, marital or child abuse can so damage self, that a second, distinct identity is developed, substituting for original self. If this identity becomes the main personality, it can become the only voice through which a person relates to the world. Original self is buried. A treasure unfortunately and repeatedly left unclaimed. Even if it's destructive, we're drawn to what we've been accustomed to, to what we've been led to believe we deserve.

I don't tell the women all this. Sometimes you can't tell people everything. They'd never believe it anyway.

I wish it had been a twenty-four hour period. One long draining day. But it was years. Different houses. And I remember each house separately, as if separate women occupied them, and all these women were walking around, never having met one another.

Our relationship was more obsession, him with me. A boxing match. Every day something happened. And if you have an abusive history you accept things. You try to please people. Or help them. We met at a poetry reading. He was a Bob Dylan type, ran away from home after dropping out of college, pretended he was insane in order to avoid the draft, wrote political poetry, created exquisite compositions on a Martin guitar, and became addicted to drugs.

The fingers of a junkie, when stoned, can curl with a rigidity that resembles death. A heroin-filled body can shut down in place like a cruel children's game of statues. The limbs become heavy; a delicate, thin body twists on linoleum in fetal position, hands grip the legs of a table, or the side of a bathtub, a burning match clutched between fingers, the smell of scorched flesh permeating the room. The body freezes and there is urgency on behalf of the onlooker, to uncurl the fingers, to prevent, if at all possible, what appears to be approaching death. The body of an addict, when filled with heroin, resembles death, and the body is walked down flights of stairs, out to the street, to regain consciousness. To walk away the madness.

We married each other one calm, clear, hopeful, and drug-free night, just the two of us, alone, under a Chinatown tree. Bought rings in a store attached to a noodle shop. It was a beautiful poem more than anything else, it certainly wasn't meant to be reality.

When I got pregnant, we married again legally. We weren't living together, we kept breaking up, and we were barely speaking. Drugs and a streak of violence were dominating everything. But at the time, in the fog of everything, it seemed the right thing to do. A friend drove us to City Hall, slowed the car along the way. He jumped out, bought gladiolas at a corner stand, and handed them to me in the middle of the

front seat, stiff paper and rubber band still attached. After the short cer-
emony he went back to his apartment and I walked alone to a coffee
shop. We should have known then, but we didn't. We were young, and
the world was falling apart.

When you have a baby growing inside you, there's this time fac-
tor. Everything happens with tremendous speed. Like an out-of-control freight train. Whistles going full blast. The stomach rises like
bread in front of your own eyes. There's another person under your
own skin, wanting out. I became an enabler. I was taking care of a
junkie and a baby, in a tiny apartment, and passing out when my
brain couldn't handle all the stress. The Cino seemed like someone
else's lifetime. Not mine.

I got dizzy in front on the apartment building one day and fell. I
remember Jack dragging me by the shoulders, along the sidewalk,
through the door, and into the hallway. And I remember an old Russian
woman with a wide white babushka looking down at me, and then
looking at Jack. I was seeing a doctor in New York for the first time. Jack
maintained I was having seizures to get attention. If this had ever been
my goal I would have chosen a very different approach.

A clean start, my idea, away from heroin. Away from drugs.
Station wagon across the Rockies. From Manhattan to Vancouver in the
hot month of July, trying not to say anything to irritate. In the front seat
with baby Heather for thousands of miles, then for a reason I will never
be able to explain, while the car was stopped at a gas station, emptied
the packed back seat partially to the front and moved abruptly to the
back with the baby. Seconds later hit by a drunk driver. Entire front passenger side demolished. Car demolished. The three of us safe.
Something invisible forced me to move. Like receiving an urgent message. "MOVE NOW!"

The Vancouver basement apartment overlooked earth and stalks
of vegetation, bicycle wheels, a child's wagon. Long periods of no
money and searching for bottles on silent, blue mornings. Exchanges
made for bread and eggs at a tiny Chinese grocery store. Breakfast for
a child. And gathering cigarette butts for a father sleeping beneath
detachment's blankets. The best places for cigarette butts are bus stops.
People light up, the bus comes and they toss the cigarette. I learned
where the stops with heavy smokers were and waited to the side as
they boarded. Then gathered the butts after the bus pulled out. Picking

bottles from the streets to exchange for food is a little like eating out of garbage cans. If this happens and if you're lucky, something snaps, like a whip and a very fast change is wanted. To anywhere.

The move from Vancouver back to New York was made in two separate trips. He left first to find a place for us to live. I followed with Heather.

Small grey isolated house in the upstate New York woods, complete with waterbed. Body and mind defeated. I felt like an animal trapped in a zoo. Fear distorts logic. A friend asked when I forgot who I was. How would I know? I'd be the last to know. The Cino mirror disappeared. Into the ground. I dug a hole and buried it myself. Pushed a shovel into the earth as if it were a sword and buried it. Gold frame and all. Tree roots sprung into the air like arteries.

Touch became violence. Beautiful friends would visit. And leave. I remained. Things were explained away. Everything can be explained away. Life within a violent environment can include isolation, intimidation, sexual and financial manipulation, and verbal abuse. It can include physical abuse and the destruction of personal property. I wore baggy clothes. No make-up. Tried to become invisible. I looked at my clothes. How many women were living in this house? Besides me? Humiliation, isolation, and abuse may be unavoidable as a child, but as an adult, it brings an embarrassment and shame that is silencing and crippling.

Drugs swim around in an addict's mind, expanding like rice in water. Violence expands with them. The connecting word linking life with violent people is the word *mistake*. It is imperative not to make a mistake. Life is lived forever on the edge. Either an outsider understands it or not. It is not incumbent upon a survivor to make anyone understand. It is incumbent upon a survivor only to survive.

In winter the one-lane road seen from a side window would be plowed like a bold finger through thick icing. And every ten feet or so, the blue shadow of a tree. The road needed people painted in, children dressed in bright snowsuits, laughing as they carried logs for a fire. It needed civilization. There was a tree on one side of the road completely cut in half, sawed down to accommodate telephone wires. I stood beside that broken tree often. Feeling its breathing, listening to its story. I think I'd been losing my mind most of my life and I didn't know what to do. So I looked at trees instead.

Across the road, and in seeing distance from another window, was a mailbox. A grey, cylinder-shaped metal box on a pole, with a moveable red metal flag. Letters replaced forbidden phone calls and their cause for violence. Sometimes when I had money, a few dollars received in a letter, I'd leave a note in the box for the mailman for stamps and flip up the red metal flag. The postman would drive by, slow down, reach in, and when he had mail, leave the flag standing. A road with a mailbox can become a silent river leaving somewhere, and leading somewhere else, a link to an outside world.

My writing changed when it existed. It became brief. Fragmented. Jumbled, like crumpled pages from a dictionary. Unrelated words next to one another.

When I found a job at a college, twenty miles away, he drove me there and picked me up. There was no public transportation in the middle of the woods. I was a switchboard operator on Sunday nights. I'd never seen a switchboard in my life. Desperate for money and the outside world, I said I'd worked a board awhile ago. Just needed some freshening up. I kept saying, "This board is really different" for days, until I finally got it. I think the woman knew all along. A look covered my face that I had no control over. Fears choking me like a scarf.

Trauma isn't a tidy thing. It echoes. Crashing over the skin like waves on a beach. Who knew the human body could hold so many tears.

Kenny, the forest creatures from *Snow White*, asked me to write about events now considered normal. He'd invite me to visit in the city. And I'd write about it, for him. I accepted and wrote in detail about two women. One in the city with friends, and another in the woods, isolated.

> 1972, March. Journal for Kenny.
>
> Train to Grand Central.
>
> Walking some parts of the Bowery is like slipping down the throat of a toilet. Kenny is home. Iron "going-uptown-to-the-opera clothes." Bathe from a bowl. Smell of oil paint drying on canvas is everywhere.
>
> Lincoln Center. Sink into velvet seats. This is where I want to stay. Invisible. Chinatown, taxi, chimes. Kenny, me, and bowls of rice.

Saturday: Watch TV horror movies. Walk with friends. Find thirty feet of twinkle lights. Just what I need!

Sunday: I turn on an extra lamp. Complete black-out at 355-1/2 Bowery. An actor named Barry Bostwick has no lights.

Manhattan is an hourglass. Time is up.

Grand Central again. Train goes backwards. Jack is waiting at the other end.

1972, July. Second journal for Kenny.

Dawn of my 29th year. Picked blackberries, pack a light bag. Away from things. Grand Central. To stay with Jack's friend, Eve, a dope seller. I take this in stride.

She has to cut five spoons of amphetamine and bag it. Three hours later we go for barley soup. Talk to Kenny on the phone. Eve is paranoid. Taxi back to her apartment.

Saturday: I wake to the sounds of women's voices. See Eve and two women shooting up. One of them is pregnant. Women leave. Eve gets off again. I make her coffee. And my second. There's no milk. A buyer phones. I try to leave. Eve complains about the state of her apartment. I vacuum for her. Clean all counters and tables. There's no soap. Leave the stack of dirty dishes. Buyer arrives. He gets off. I have to get out. Buy flowers and visit a friend. We talk about little things. Make candles. Have tea. Eve arrives. We see a play Kenny has given me tickets for.

Eve won't stop talking. I'm drained. Little sleep. Minimum of food. Found out a friend had committed suicide and another had died from some kind of poisoned blood. Am drained and quiet. Eve interprets this as boredom with her and is hostile. I tell her we should leave the theatre.

Back in the apartment I sit on the floor with my head buried in my hands.

Tension. 5 A.M. Black coffee. She asks me to stop being rude. I can't deal with the amphetamine talk. I

tell her she's scared. We are screaming at one another
at the top of our lungs.

At 5:30 in the morning I start to leave. She screams
obscenities and fingers a razor blade, then dramatically
locks herself in the bathroom and screams how terrible
I am.

I pick up my things, including a small artificial
Christmas tree I found, and leave.

Train to Poughkeepsie.

While Jack drives me to the college where I work,
I kiss Heather, change clothes in the moving car, sink in
front of a switchboard, with a coffee with milk in it, a
Danish and no mind.

"Hello…hello…hello."

Documentation became the first step towards a bridge from madness. A neon sign pointing OUT. Months later, good friends came to visit
with a car. When we were married at City Hall they'd been our witnesses. Now they were witnesses again. I left a note on the round table
by the window telling him where I'd gone and asked him to join us.
Dinner at their house. Talk about relocation. Near people.

When he got home and found the note, he phoned.

"How did you get out?" he asked, "How did you get out?"

I'd been living in some bizarre form of captivity. If people are
treated in an insane manner, long enough, there's a good chance they'll
become insane.

I made the decision to move from the isolated grey house so fast
there were skid marks on the sky. Relocation to a small town.
Newspapers. On the way from the parking lot to a newspaper stand, a
cardboard sign on a wall: APARTMENT FOR RENT UPSTAIRS: SEE MARKY INSIDE.
The move began that night. Birds flew in all directions. I became an
exploding gasoline truck. An out-of-control asteroid. Walls with holes
punched into them, left behind. I set fire to every memory. Imaginary
flames spilled as we pulled from the driveway. Everything torched.
Child on one arm. Fire on the other. Nothing is spared. My mind saw
only red. Ashes fell where previously there had been terror. Everything
was on fire. Everything torched with imaginary matches. Nothing
remained except the ruins. I became fire.

Abuse of other human beings is against the law. Isolation does not change that fact. I could have died there. Or I could have died trying to leave. I chose the latter. I didn't die.

New house. Three of us living over a pinball palace. I listened to the sounds of air hockey pucks slamming against the sides of machines at night. Other people's violence. He painted the kitchen blood-red enamel. And wedged a birch tree, with branches severed, between the floor and ceiling. A limbless, rootless slaughtered birch in the middle of a blood-red kitchen. I may have decided to make the move. But he was deciding what life would be like there. Blood-red kitchen and the blue Cino cup smashed on the floor.

Jack's frightening violence was escalating and we were barely speaking again. The kitchen was a mess from him the night before. Excessive clutter and noise made me extremely nervous, as if it were consuming me. I began to clean up the mess, and then lost control of my breathing. Wanted to do something but felt as if breath was being sucked out of me and I fell. I could hear Heather talking to me. I think I was answering her in the middle of passing out.

Except for never-ending headaches, after a cup of tea and a twenty-four-hour radio station, things seemed normal again. I called this normal. A post office was in walking distance. Everyone a postage stamp away. A flag pole surrounded by thick granite benches, a town bus stop, two health food stores, hardware store, a deli, a circle of pebbles in the park—somebody's altar, a mailbox, a stop sign, traffic, windows overlooking church weddings, grey and melon skies, a community rock garden—violets with wild things.

One year later, a second house with a rickety sundeck, big trees, and no man in the house. Legal separation. Repetitive trauma in adult life eats away at a formed personality. Repetitive trauma in childhood deforms a personality. By now, who had I become? I walked with my hands tied across my stomach in a knot. When people asked why I walked that way, I told them I was trying to hold myself together and they left me alone. He'd drive past in his green pickup truck, watching. No words were spoken. None needed. I felt as if he were waiting for me to mess up. At night, awake and alone, under my own covers, in the quiet, I was still on guard. It was all the layers of different kinds of trauma. Brush strokes on canvas. Layers of thick paint piled on top of trees.

One summer I was under so much stress, from Jack, from everything, I passed out in the middle of town. On the pavement. Looked up from the concrete. Little white things lying in a pool of red. Reached into the blood. Picked up the broken pieces of my teeth. Walked the long road home up the mountain. Alone. Lips tightly closed. Mouth flooding with blood. Too embarrassed to spit. The dentist said I looked as if someone had beaten me with a baseball bat. It was a bat. A psychological bat. And a different drug. An experiment. After four horrific weeks I took myself off it. A nightmare. Doctors know if something doesn't work only after you've gone insane. There are two separate kinds of trauma. Trauma to the mind and trauma to the body. Sometimes we find ourselves dealing with both simultaneously. Went back to original medication. More herb tea, meditation, and books on mental healing. Mysticism.

A myriad of jobs. Supermarkets, school buses, babysitters, the smell of dandelion on back roads and people walking slowly. Sounds of a jacket sleeve writing across a page. Crying silently in the dark. Wondering and worrying. Lighting candles and hoping. Homemade soup and a dozen ways to make lentils. Children in raincoats, waiting for a bus. Christmas on a village green. January snow at sunset. Full moons over a quiet town at midnight. Collecting the words written on the edges of paper. The smell of mittens drying. Halloween and trick-or-treaters. A cat waiting patiently for food. A bus in front of the house. Gregorian chants from a supermarket radio. A strong daughter in junior high. Curtains blowing back and forth, a pale blue sky with long, thin clouds. Collage work and the local art scene. Shredded paper, lace, and shiny things. A one-woman show. Stepping slowly from darkness.

The desire to survive is rarely completely extinguished. The desire to get to the other side, to community, is as vital as breathing. For years I corresponded with every strong person I'd ever known. Some in close proximity. Others halfway across the world. The wonder of strength and courage passed from one soul to another, across borders and through walls, still astounds me. The memories from my past are unchangeable. I can't unown them. They're mine. Like a dark grey crystal ball I carry around inside me. Rolling around silently and smooth from my head to my feet. No matter how much light I expose it to, it remains impenetrable. Unchangeable. This dark ball I carry around is as much a part of me as my shoulder or my heart. It lives in my heart. Innocent. Like a feather, or a switchblade.

The woman I am becoming at this complex of buildings has the complexities of at least four different voices thinking simultaneously. One of them, maybe all of them, wants to smile again. To walk to no place in particular and be home at no time especially. Wants to learn to speak without crying. A new voice is emerging. Inside me. And it's moving with a speed torn from the wings of angels who've been standing around doing nothing. The body heals more rapidly than the mind. But with the right environment, they can heal together. A group of nuns in the woods have noticed me. And are responding.

All of the women had heard stories of abuse and violence. Nothing is unmentionable with them. They are like wings for one another and now they've included me. They speak about people they know, people who are trapped, and those who've moved away from terror.

In the evening after dinner, some of us meet on the veranda again, then each of us drifts off with our own private thoughts. Some return to their rooms in the complex, some walk together on the paths surrounding the main house, and a few of us walk separately to the meadow in the approaching dusk. The wild half of the meadow, below the cliff, is barely visible.

As the sky darkens, women who are in the meadow begin to leave. But before they do, each says good night, a way of letting me know perhaps that I am about to be alone. But I'm not finished with the meadow yet. I'm not ready to leave this place where all week, time seemed to be going backwards and forwards, where unexplained forces have transpired, where everything seems to be filled with power and so I sit in the darkness and silence, alone, with only the wind and sky. And the unceasing stream of images going through my mind.

Where have I been? Who have I been for half a century?

In one week everything is suddenly different, as if I've snapped my fingers, taken myself out of a trance. All memories overlap, all indistinguishable. There is only this new moment. And the possibility of ley lines. People must be attracted to certain locations on the globe for a reason. It makes sense that these locations would be lined up with one another.

At this complex, in one week, my entire life has changed slightly. Like antique silk. Like my blue shawl with stars of now tarnished sequins. My first Mother's Day gift, from people at the Caffe Cino. Fragile material, not something for warmth. I need thick blankets wrapped around me now. Knees and feet tucked under. I'm like a child just home from a skating party, freezing from wind on an icy pond. I want to make hot chocolate and tell myself a story. Put my toes in front of the oven. Want someone to hold me. Someone to say, "I love you," and really mean it. But I'm alone in the woods with nuns. And the memories are flying in all directions like birds at the sound of gunshot.

I return to the complex, punch the secret code into the locked door, walk through the silent hallways to my room, and go to sleep.

I dream I'm alone on a long road. It's twilight in my dream. The sky is dark blue ink and peppered with stars, all shapes, and all colours. Some are shooting across cloud formations and there is peace.

I walk a long time on this empty road, surrounded by mountains, never seeing any traveller, even in the distance. And I'm not afraid. Occasionally a bird can be seen. Except for the birds and the stars and the mountains, there is nothing. Except the road. And me walking on it. Alone. I can hear my own footsteps. An even, steady pace, like breathing in and breathing out. Each footstep on this empty road is like a breath. As night grows darker in my dream, buildings begin to appear on either side of the road. Some are lit with candles, some are dark, and some have tiny lights outlining a structure. Tiny lights against a stone-grey mountain, beneath dark blue sky.

People begin to appear. Slowly. As if they're being painted in with a fine brush, one part of the anatomy at a time. On one side of the road are people who have knowingly or unknowingly caused pain. The knowledge is irrelevant. Pain happens if it's inflicted. These people are brushed into existence on one side of the road only. And I walk past them without hesitation. Without fear or pain.

On the opposite side of the road, other people are being brushed into existence. The faces of all the people from the Caffe Cino in the 1960s, people who've taught me about magic. Anyone who has ever entered my life and brought happiness, all of them gradually appear, fade-in to existence. And except for the birds and the stars and the mountains, there is nothing. Except the road I'm walking on and people on either side, like trees in a forest. Those who've caused pain on one side and those who've brought happiness on the other. It is clear in my dream that these are two completely different groups of people. And both groups are where they belong. I continue walking slowly, on the empty road, through this forest of people, with buildings on either side, and I feel myself holding my own heart in my own hands which are small, and my heart is swollen and large and heavy. This heavy heart needed to be held for a long time. It needed to be walked, like a small child. It needed vigilance. And wisdom. And a safe new beginning. While holding the heaviness of my own heart in my own hands, I continue to walk on the empty road, through the forest of people, towards a clear and certain destination, a pinpoint on a map, without hesitation. Everyone who has ever lived in my lifetime, or been a part of my lifetime, is on one side of the empty road or the other. And there is complete and total order. Harmony. There is no competition to get from one side of the road to the other. To even speak or move. People stand calmly like trees, each in their proper place. And in my dream I walk calmly down this quiet road. Forever.

I wake in the middle of the night, parched, like someone in a desert. Maybe my brain is taking the opportunity to organize a very chaotic lifetime.

The moon tonight is hidden. It's somewhere above The Queen of Peace Room. The air is drenched with memories. There are no stars, only clouds and wind. I decide to wait. In time a patch of blue might appear, and I want to make a wish.

Pigeons, whales, and honeybees can navigate using the earth's magnetic field. The physiological feature that enables them to do this is a tissue with a substance called magnetite in it. Magnetite enables them to sense magnetic changes and has been found in human tissue associated with the Ethmoid bone in front of the vertebrate skull.

— T. Williamson, "A Sense of Direction for Dowsers?"

Homing pigeons find their way home by tuning into the earth's field by crystals of the magnetic mineral magnetite located on the surface of their brains. This magnetic organ enables them to navigate their way home through darkness and fog.

— Daniel Reid, *The Complete Book of Chinese Health and Healing*

WEDNESDAY, PRE-DAWN

The tree outside the window is at peace after last night's battle with the wind. Only a few leaves have been lost in the storm. I don't feel tired even though I've gotten only a few hours sleep. If anything, just the opposite. There is a subtle shift in the light in the sky, a subtle shift to gold blue. The sun is rising. A long-winged bird flies swiftly, like a skater. A long row of black birds fly together, like nuns. Like a large connected family. Everything is ready for the new day.

We meet in the meadow, as we've been doing all week, and then walk up the hill to the dining room and breakfast. At 9 A.M. we meet in the main house again. People speak about the earth, the environment, about AIDS, and how it affects families. Sisters who've worked in African villages or knew sisters who have, speak as if they've truly seen the inside rooms of hell.

Sitting by the bedside of someone in the last months of AIDS is like watching clouds over the sun. You wait for the clouds to pass. Sometimes it's overcast for weeks. Then one day, like a miracle, there's sunshine and things are clear, normal, and the way they used to be. It may last for only a minute, an hour if you're lucky. But most of the time is spent waiting. Beneath the layers of blanket is a person who once shared your hopes and dreams. Beneath all that cloud, the old familiar person still exists. Beneath the swelling and bruises and sores is someone you love. But it's all concealed. Changed by tubing, dementia, adult-sized diapers, and food that doesn't require chewing. And blinking metal boxes attached through wires to a leg or arm.

These machines embrace the body now the way a lover once did. But the feeling is cold. Metallic. It gives the body no warmth. And this is what the person in the last weeks of AIDS needs. Body heat. To be held. To be whispered to. Sung to. Read to. The machines and tubes and plastic sheets and tissues for everyone's tears, are all part of the final moments. A Rolex ticking on bone.

No one had any way of knowing that the timing of the Caffe Cino exhibition at Lincoln Center in 1985 would be so ominous. The Research Library wanted me to curate an exhibit on the Caffe and the roots of Off-Off Broadway. I moved back to New York City and we spent two years looking for documentation. People trusted us with wrinkled posters, pieces of costumes, and things from the wall. Kenny recreated the entire Caffe kitchen. It came together like a wild jigsaw puzzle. The exhibit opened in 1985 at the Astor Gallery. The walls contained hundreds of photos by Jimmy Gossage. Thousands of facts, fragments, lists of plays performed, names of playwrights, directors, actors, designers, Pulitzer Prize winners, their training done on a tiny piece of wood, payment in coffee and a sandwich and whatever was collected from the basket passed nightly to the audience. A concealed electric fan recreated the breeze that once drifted through the room; it shook wind chimes and the sound blended with a tape of Kate Smith and Callas. Shirley Temple, calliope music, "Silent Night," and Mozart. It was almost like walking through the Caffe door. There was even a piece of the door in a glass case. God knows where it came from, who'd been holding onto it all that time. It just appeared one day. Like the Caffe itself. We'd pieced together the only history of the Caffe and Off-Off Broadway that will probably ever exist. The passion and wildness were at Lincoln Center for three months. On opening night there were 1,500 people in a space designed for 500. It was Caffe Cino/Off-Off Broadway gridlock. Rhinestones, Wonder Woman, sequins, bad plaid, tuxedos, and Italian pastries all clashing with one another. But within a three-year period, twenty-three friends had either died or were dying from AIDS. Cino people died in an unrelenting, merciless succession. It felt like Vietnam, except I knew people inside the body bags intimately. Kenny in one hospital room and Neil in another. I brought a basket of crystals to Neil and avocados to Kenny. Kenny wanted to stop wasting away. To get fat. He'd always been practical. Nothing worked. Rubber gloves, face masks, knives to cut food into tiny pieces, straws for tiny paper cups that were easy to lift, blinking medical equipment, nothing worked. Everyone was dying. I gave Kenny lists of fattening foods. Food that couldn't be eaten because it couldn't be swallowed. We exchanged the letters anyway. They contained the memory of the avocado sliding past the throat. A nurse on the AIDS ward kept these letters visible. Any reading could be the last supper. Kenny had been in the hospital three times. Approaching death was calculated by how many times a person had been hospitalized.

He spent the last weeks of his life dying next to a stranger. A skeletal man named Danny. The two of them separated by a thin hospital curtain. Both of them slipping in and out of dementia. Both of them yelling at the other when they had the strength. Arguing over who had used the phone and awakened the other. Neither of them remembering who had done what. The mind playing vicious games. If it weren't so unbearably tragic, it might have been funny. Danny stared at a bowl of won ton soup, brought in by a nurse on a lunch break. The bowl seemed nearly as big as his head. And Kenny, an artist obsessed with colour, completely blind in both eyes, in a state of dementia, fumbling for non-existent brushes. The last weeks of AIDS are about surrender. Of everything.

There was a tall thin closet in Kenny's room, across from his pillow. Hidden inside were extra bottles of AZT and vials of experimental medicine gotten at personal risk by friends. Johnny and I walked silently through the hospital hallway one night. I had the bag of medication from the closet in my hand and handed it to him, to add to his own arsenal. Kenny could no longer swallow. Neither of us spoke. What words could we possibly have used?

Another friend went to Mexico with his dying lover in search of cures. His lover died just after they'd crossed the border. Alone now, with a dead body in the car, and terrified of customs, he left his lover's body in the Mexican desert and returned to New York alone. No one tells you how to explain these things to customs.

The mind becomes a cluttered jewellery box, a lid unable to close, bulging with images and memories.

The Cino people, despite their wildness, or maybe because of their wildness, were my entire extended family. They were the collective Royal Huntsman. Anyone can be a Prince, you only need to be handsome and own a horse, but a Huntsman needs to be courageous, very quick thinking, and kind. It's always been my opinion that he was the true hero of that story.

In 1988 Heather and I constructed seven heart-breaking panels for the AIDS Memorial Quilt, and mailed them away to be sewn into the main massive quilt. The following year, I constructed Kenny's alone, and brought it by train to the display in Washington, DC. It was raining that year and I made the exchange on a wide avenue in the pouring rain with a volunteer worker dressed in white. I tried to think of a song that reminded me of this desperate emptiness. But I couldn't. It hadn't been written. I was alone in the rain, Kenny-less, and dozens of friends were dying. Needles, facemasks, IVs, bandages, clipboards with pages of useless information, were all part of a sacrifice for some invisible monster, instiable in its hunger for bodies.

According to legend, Jesus wiped his face on a shawl the day he was carrying a wooden cross up a mountain to his death. A woman named Veronica stepped out of the crowd and offered her shawl to the man with a bleeding face. When Jesus returned the shawl, according to legend, it contained the stained and bloodied image of his face, preserved to this day in the vault of a cathedral. The world's first Xerox copy.

I wanted an image of the monster that consumed my friends. I wanted a Xerox copy of its face the way Jesus gave Veronica a copy. I want the empty pages in my phone book explained to me, addresses now marked *heaven*.

No amount of sunflowers, expensive tiny chocolates, potted plants that required little watering, or balloons saying "We Love You"; no amount of holy cards, or visiting hours that no one really obeyed at this stage of the game, no amount of crystals tied to ID bracelets, no amount of coughing that sounded as if it were coming from the depths of the earth itself; no amount of rage beneath the skin of the person in the bed, or the skin of the person at the edge of the bed, could reverse this situation and I wanted a Xerox copy of the violent monster responsible. I wanted my friends back.

The 1980s were about death. Anyone who didn't die in the 60s, died in the 80s. The 70s were simply pinned together with violence.

Heather graduated from high school with Honours. In 1988 Jack drank himself to death. The last we saw of him was a brown paper bag of belongings, folded shut by a hospital worker. A shaving brush, a pill bottle, and a toothbrush. He died in a hospital while we were on our way to see him. He left one tiny poem for us. About sorrows and falling leaves. And how they both ought to pass away, quietly.

The child who waited one Christmas Eve in coat and scarf, holding gifts for a father who never appeared, who fell asleep on the sofa, clutching presents and ribbons, grew into a woman who turned her back on people. Occasionally. Including me.

The girl who saw her father die young in his forties, then helped write his obituary, who saw her godfather die from AIDS the next year, and five years later saw her boyfriend, a man many years her senior, die from a brain tumour, knew the smell of death better than a young person should. It permeated her clothes. It seeped into her bones. It threatened to engulf her sometimes. The child who learned to tap dance and sing, and loved music, grew into a woman who studied musicians on the fringes of life. The outcasts, the rebels, the misfits. People with their own violent past. Their own haunted houses.

I hope a day will come when violence has ended. Not because it's been outlawed but because no one enjoys it anymore. Grown weary of the sight of blood drops, would rather go for a long walk instead. Splash their toes in river water. Watch the drops catch the sunlight. Maybe go home and knit. Learn to purl.

NO!

The needles could be used as weapons.

Just walk.

And I do. In the late morning and all afternoon. I feel like a snake removing its skin. Layer by layer by layer. Like an awkward package at a lost and found, waiting to be claimed. Wanting to be calm. The electronic bulletin board in my head wants to be turned off. No more images flashing. Times Square has been flashing its electronic zipper since 1928. It was dark for only two years in the 1960s. I want mine stopped.

Thoughts and memories are lodged inside my cells. Some have been living there for almost half a century. I have to split my self in half, just as the meadow is split in half, and allow all the poison to drain. In order to remove the pain, I have to first remove the memory.

Late in the afternoon we're given an assignment. To go into nature and look for a sign of ourselves.

I wander around the complex, on the paths and wooden trails, then down the hill to the meadow, and finally down the cliff and into the middle of the lower, wild meadow. Sister Norma's socks tucked over my jeans, through the wild uncut part, past indentations in the grass where wild animals had slept the night before. Or maybe even minutes before. I see only the indentations. I sit on the ground, place my walkman and the voice of Ferron in the tall wild weeds and ask the earth to show me myself in nature. Nothing exists except stillness.

I wait and watch in silence as a delicate, solitary, black and blue butterfly lands on a tall blade of grass directly in front of me.

Transformation.

After dinner, with warm winds creaking around us and an evening quiet settling in, we talk about the future.

The future I saw came in a dream.

Stars are easier to identify. The L-shaped Scorpio and the kite-shaped Libra. There's water, but people use it cautiously. Newspapers have changed. Some trees still exist, with fences around them. People look at trees the way we once looked at animals in a zoo. The wind exists but has enormous power. The sun can now do severe damage to the skin, so people do things at night. All office hours are in the evening. People shop for food under stars, children by their side. People walk with babies at midnight in what resembles a park. We have finally taken back the night, but I don't think this is what we had in mind. Art galleries open at midnight.

All schools have only night hours. Everything is the same yet different. Adjustment. Then it all seems normal.

One thing never changed. Snow. How it changes the chemistry of a population. People slow down. They look at space around the snow. Where it fell. They play, or think about play.

Few people watch television. There was a time when that's all people did. Go to work. Come home. Watch TV. Some even watched at work, on inconspicuous sets.

In the future, people pay more attention to the weather. Not the weather on television, but the real weather. The food supply depends on it. Killer germs are influenced by it. The entranceway to large cities depends on the weather. And it changes too fast to be recorded. Television can tell you only about the past.

Wind travels with a fury and things get dusty.

Bird sounds are recorded and traded. People watch for birds in the pre-dawn hours after work, or after they've picked children up from night school. People still toss crumbs to birds in small towns. It's been outlawed in large cities. An attempt at sanitation.

Wars have stopped. People are too busy finding food, working in soup kitchens, or cleaning the dust. Occasional disturbances are settled by small groups of people who are diplomatic. They're not diplomats, just diplomatic. People save seeds when they eat fresh produce. We used to throw millions of seeds away daily. Now they're carefully laid in the sun to dry. It's hard to believe this was once considered garbage.

People are no longer defined by what they do. Everyone can cook. Mend a shirt. Teach children. Heal a wound. Build an altar. People have learned to survive in the future, in my dream.

I saw whole books written in my dreams, except the pens turned into forks and spoons and I couldn't record anything. Some of it had to do with church and women and men. But the words are gone. They flutter like strands of ribbon on a clothesline. Some were in Latin and I understood it. And some of the words had to do with prayer and change.

I dreamt that a donkey caught the carrot on a stick. Everyone was surprised. Especially those who'd called it a stupid ass.

Later at night, moons whiz by like fireflies. They move in the sky between clouds, sliding in and out of view as if they are hiding behind white-layered curtains, like performers, then reappear through an invisible seam. Layers of moons against layers of blue.

This is the sky on Wednesday night.

Five hundred or so miles south of Cuzco, lines criss-cross the altiplano of Western Bolivia. Some of these lines are twenty miles long, considerably longer than any found at Nazca. French anthropologist Alfred Metraux came across them in the 1930s when he investigated earthen shrines set out in a straight row from a small village. He found them to be standing on a pathway that was "absolutely straight, regardless of the irregularities of the road."

— Paul Devereux, *The Long Trip*

THURSDAY, 9 A.M.

After finishing breakfast with the women on the retreat, I realize that the overwhelming power of love is more healing than any medication, any inoculation, any amount of money, any vacation to any resort. Love in its truest form can move mountains. In its most honest form can let the silenced speak and can, in its wisest form, teach love to others—so that they in turn may teach it.

Why would anyone ever want to suppress this power? Why would anyone want to deny this healing to our world today?

In the evening, in the meeting house at this strange complex of buildings in the woods, where on the day of my arrival I heard a voice say, "All things that are supposed to meet, will eventually meet," angels give me a birthday party, and the sounds of nuns singing in Latin at Saint Henry's Church in the 1950s, echo. Except there are no leather straps here, no knives in my face, or the threats of knives, no judgments being made. Only singing, guitar music, dancing, and laughter. And a tiny table filled with food. Gentleness. Caring. Laughter in moonlight. A small night party with nuns in the woods. I am allowed to become whoever it is I am to become. And a gift. A blank book. With delicate handmade pages, for new memories, different ones.

At the end of the evening, after cleaning up, we lower the windows, leave the meeting house, and return to our separate rooms in the main building.

Inside the complex, most of us take the stairs instead of the elevator. Two of the sisters ask if I'd like to assist in the early morning mass in the chapel, especially since it's going to be my fiftieth birthday. I hesitate, fearful that I'll make a terrible mistake—set fire to the altar cloth, spill the wine, drop the bread, forget something. They assure me that such mistakes aren't possible. Sister Mary will be there, coaching me along. I say a reluctant but happy yes, and we say good night.

When I get to my room, two birthday cards have been pushed under my door.

I splash cold water on my face, put on the white nightgown, wipe the tears I'm ashamed of crying, and turn out the lights in The Queen of Peace Room. Every sister is resting. Every sister except me.

My eyes won't shut. Even when I close them, they may as well be open. I can still see everything. The meadow. The sky. The dining room. The chapel with its marble focused Mary. The circle of strong caring women. Their comfortable shoes. Their tender eyes. Their gentle voices.

Finally I fall asleep and dream.

I'm standing with a blue vision I've dreamt about before. And she speaks:

"I'm going now to the place where the white stars end and the tiny red ones begin. To the place where clouds are golden and shaped like leaves from a tree, where one white enormous star shines in a pool of dark blue velvet sky. I will return often. You will see me. Be aware of the sky. Listen to the sky. Watch for the gentleness of love drifting overhead in the shape of the morning sun. Underneath, in a blade of grass. In the millions of stars, a needle on a bough. A snowflake on a window. Look for these things. Truly see these things and I will be there. Watch for lights to shift in the sky from pink to gold to black and you will see me. I will be in every small flower. In every snow-capped mountain. Look for me. If things get rough, reach out, far. Extend your hand beyond the edge of the cliff. I will be there. Always. And there will be times when you do not call and I will reappear anyway. And those moments will be occasions of great joy. We will dance and sing. And you will laugh out loud. You will see. Trust what I am saying."

I watch her walk into the air and vanish like a flame in water.

The Hopewell (150 B.C.-A.D. 500) built burial mounds and huge, geometrical earthworks, including circular and hexagonal enclosed areas covering many acres, and giant earthen mounds and truncated pyramids, along with linear features that seem to have been ceremonial roadways...

In 1995, Bradley T. Lepper, curator of archaeology at the Ohio Historical Society, announced the finding of even more extensive Hopewell linear sacred geography. He has evidence that a sixty-mile long Hopewell ceremonial road connected modern Newark and Chillicothe in a straight line across the Ohio countryside.

— Paul Devereux, *The Long Trip*

FRIDAY. RAIN.

In the very early morning I walk alone under my black umbrella, which actually belongs to a Canadian poet. He left it at my apartment, so I'm thinking of him in the heavy rain, in these woods, in this gentle silence, and I have another revelation.

The voice of Jesus is speaking to me and He says, "I'll take care of the crying—you take care of the writing."

Without hesitation I say into the air, "Deal!"

These are His tears. I can't cry like this. This is what I'm thinking, alone in the rain, on my fiftieth birthday. Jesus is offering consolation, the way He consoled Veronica on the way to that terrible mountain.

"Deal," I say.

This is how I reply to the voice of Jesus. My one face-to-face, or voice-to-voice contact and this is how I respond.

Deal!

The rain continues. It doesn't stop for hours. The only day in eight that it's rained. On the seventh day God rested, but on the eighth day God cried.

A rabbit, large black eyes, tenses as I near and then scuttles under leaves. Fearful. But there are no traps here. Only grass, now soft and wet.

Up in my room, I put the dripping umbrella in the bathtub, change into dry clothes and prepare to assist Sister Mary in the chapel.

I wear my long white lace scarf as a revolutionary act against the Pope for not ordaining women. All women should wear white lace scarves if they want equality. It could be a secret code.

In the chapel I have four things to remember. Light the candle. Bring plates from a sideboard to the altar. Help Sister Mary tear bread into tiny pieces. Then say four words to the group, "The table is ready."

I watch for her signal, her eyes telling me when to leave my seat. We walk up together as she whispers directions under her breath. As I light the large, single white candle in the middle of the altar, I realize it's my birthday. I want to make a wish. But for what? I've had a conversation with Jesus. Challenged the Pope in writing. Am wearing my revolutionary lace on the altar, and been dancing and singing with angels. Angels who don't have complicated names. They have simple names like Eileen and Mary, Norma and Theresa, Jayne, Katie and Mille, Christine, Eleanor, Johannah, Elena, Marie, and Joan.

I've been given the gift of a new beginning at this complex. I carry dishes from a sideboard, help tear the bread into tiny pieces, and then turn to go back to my seat. Sister Mary touches me gently on the arm.

"The table is ready," she whispers to me almost inaudibly. I knew it!

"The table is ready," I say as I turn and face the group.

Our bodies remember every experience. The love in this room has moved a mountain. The one standing on my chest, crushing me. This mountain of violence, abuse, deaths, of drugged and drunken rages, has begun to dissolve. Like ice outside a refrigerator. Like night. This is why I was to stay here. To remember. To begin to feel loved. Light and heat, two intangible factors that control every move we make, every day of our lives. Love is also intangible.

Because I haven't planned the week in advance, The Queen of Peace Room is reserved for Friday night. I'm moved to a cell-like cubicle on a vacant upper floor. My real needs are defined even further. Writing, stones, bark, and a candle, my only things on a small wooden table. I sit alone on the narrow bed, in the quiet, and rest my back against the cold stone wall. I could be a woman in any country, any century.

By Saturday, we've all gone our separate ways.

I say goodbye to these gentle women reluctantly. I long to hold onto them, but they're like shapes made from dew on the morning grass. They dissolve before my eyes. Most of them in Friday's rain. Goodbye over corn muffins and they vanish.

I walk down to the meadow one last time and stand at the fringe, letting the wind that blows across it fill my hair, and I take one long last picture to keep forever, in my mind, of the meadow and the trees surrounding everything.

Trees are constantly bending towards the light. We can learn a lot from trees.

Epilogue

Stillness allows us to think whatever we dare to think. It waits as we sort through all the circumstances that make up what yesterday was. It rests in containers piled high like canned pears on a shelf. There is no electricity, wind is the only music. The moon and stars, a source of light. All things may look like blood. But they aren't. They're red stars. And petals from a rose. Stillness involves waiting. For the fog to lift. And it will. In time, everything becomes a memory. In time, everything is washed away, including the blood of John the Baptist.

Stillness waits as we decide what we'll think about. What we'll do with our time, who will be our friends. We wait in the stillness until we realize we must face the present. The future is far. The past is gone. There is only this present, to cherish. To cherish the eyes of night. Eyes, too numerous to count.

Stillness exists in the space around things, if things are given enough space. It exists in a candle glowing in a glass holder, a bird on a branch, people's eyes, in the beauty of nature.

I willed to believe in the power and stillness of a meadow to work me through half a century of madness. I willed to believe; and in so doing, whether ley lines were present or not, I willed it and the surrounding complex to be an unending source of strength and permission.

Permission to be brave, to hope, to be strong.

Permission to write what I didn't want to speak. To honour my own words. To move without question, without boundaries, without apologies, to live without stigma.

Permission to create, to be happy, to live in peace.
Permission to look at trees and see companions.
Permission to honour complexity. To shatter darkness.
Conclusion. Without judgment.

WORKS CITED

"All About Acupuncture." <www.AcupunctureToday.com> November 2001.

The American Heritage Dictionary of the English Language. 3rd ed. Boston: Houghton Mifflin, 1982.

Caldicott, Helen. *Missile Envy.* New York: Bantam, 1986.

Devereux, Paul. *The Long Trip.* New York: Penguin Putnam, 1997.

Lannon, Alice, and Mike McCarthy. *Fables, Fairies and Folklore of Newfoundland.* St. John's: Jesperson Press, 1991.

Lin, Henry B. *The Art and Science of Feng Shui.* St. Paul, MN: Lleaellyn, 2000.

The Oxford English Dictionary. Oxford: Clarendon Press, 1989.

Reid, Daniel. *The Complete Book of Health and Healing.* Boston: Shambhala, 1994.

Robin, Allen. "A New Age Dawns for Science." *New Scientist,* 14 December 1991, 52.

Sullivan, Danny. *Ley Lines: A Comprehensive Guide to Alignments.* Cited in "The Ley of the Land" by David Newham. *The Guardian,* 13 May 2000.

Too, Lillian. *The Fundamentals of Feng Shui.* Boston: Element Books, 1999.

Williamson, T. "A Sense of Direction for Dowsers?" *New Scientist,* 19 March 1987.

READING *THE QUEEN OF PEACE ROOM* AS WITNESS: AN ETHICS OF ENCOUNTER

SHARON ROSENBERG

Testimonial projects that involve narrating that which breaks
the frame require...a listener no less than a speaking subject.

— Gilmore 2001: 31

Magie Dominic and I have never met in person, never spoken on the phone or exchanged an e-mail. We do not live in the same city; we are born of different generations, and we carry different familial legacies. And yet her story haunts me, reverberates across the skin of my life, traces of her telling left behind in my psyche long after I've come to her last sentence, the (temporary) end of our textual encounter. As I begin this writing, immersed in ideas about what I might say, I am deeply aware of the burden of this speech—Magie Dominic's, of course, but also, differently, mine. The weight of Dominic's burden lies most heavily, I expect, with what it means to bear public witness to her life in and through this self-representation, *The Queen of Peace Room*.[1] My burden, as an invited commentator (and, by extension, all of ours, as readers), lies with an ethic of encounter, of what it means to respectfully take in her words, carry her witness beyond the moment of my (and our) engagement, and speak to the larger social truths that she evidences here—without losing sight of what she reminds us of so well: the specificities

---

1 In this essay, I use the broad term "self-representation," rather than the more usual, "autobiography" or "life writing." In doing so, I am compelled by Leigh Gilmore's reliance on this term. She argues that trauma pushes conventions of autobiography to their limit, and, in so doing, suggests a rethinking of this form and practice (2001).

and complexities of a life cannot be reduced to what any one of us thinks we already know (Caruth 1995; Felman and Laub 1992; Simon, Rosenberg, and Eppert 2000). In tracing the contours of an ethic of encounter with Dominic's *The Queen of Peace Room*, I will provide some commentary on the character of witnessing that is involved, the grammars of violence that are evident, the nature of trauma, how Dominic responds to her experiences, and the act of her self-representation.

Although I name the reading and writing practices at issue here as marked by a burden, I mean that not in its negative sense of (too much) weight, trouble, a hindrance, or a torment, but instead as a responsibility of the reader who is called upon to not only read as a "scholar" but also as a "witness." As a scholar, I am expected to read from some (emotional) distance, to read with a certain skepticism toward claims of veracity. But as a witness, I am called upon to engage the tactility of this writing, to be open to the potentially reconfiguring effects of its knowledge. For this is a text that asks us to learn not simply the "facts" of Dominic's life, but something of the emotional, visceral, and psychological meanings and legacies of those facts (Britzman 1998): what it has meant to this woman, to her life, to have been repeatedly sexually abused as a child by a grandfather; assaulted, raped, and stalked by a man unknown to her; isolated and controlled by another man to whom she was married, with whom she had a daughter. And layered in between all of this, we encounter images of trees that vomit, a sky that waits, stars as eyes that do not turn away, a meadow marked by ley lines, Off-Off Broadway companions who make nightly magic on a shoestring at Caffe Cino, and angels taking the form of nuns. In this complexity of traumatic self-representation, Dominic may be viewed, in Leigh Gilmore's phrasing, "not so much as asking to be believed, as asserting [her] speech" (2001: 37), a speech that, from the perspective of those who harmed her, should never have come into existence.

Before I read for the specificities of what Dominic asserts here, I want to step back a moment to briefly sketch a broader sense of the everyday/every-night "gendered grammars of violence" (Marcus 1992: 392), violation, harm, isolation, and dependency of which Dominic's account gives evidence. Her experiences do not occur in a social void, but, instead, are what is risked when one is part of a family, enters adult relationships, goes to school, lives in a city. Not markers of all that happens there, or, indeed, what will happen to all people there, but it is the very everydayness of Dominic's experiences that must worry us (Brown 1995). As sociology professors Ann Duffy and Rina Cohen observe: "there is considerable evidence that, particularly in the family, women [and girls] have been targeted for victimization" (2001: 135). In the context of "the family"—that social configuration that is normatively represented as a safe haven—Duffy and Cohen identify a series of distinct yet interconnected practices: sexual abuse, physical abuse, wife abuse, marital rape, intimate femicide. They continue: "the inescapable conclusion from [a] growing body of data is that one in eight girls growing up in Canada today will likely be a victim of serious sexual abuse, and that the perpetrator will in all likelihood be male, usually a male known to the victim and in some position of authority over the victim" (136, citing Bagley and King, Gadd). As Dominic's text reminds us, violences against women also occur in non-intimate contexts; the numbers here are also disconcerting. Duffy and Cohen note a 1993 Statistics Canada survey that found "23 percent [of 12,300 women surveyed] had been subject to violent attack by a stranger" (143). They add an important note to this sentence that reads: "since many women are subject to multiple victimization—that is, they are victimized on more than one occasion and/or by more than one attacker—they have been victims of both stranger and acquaintance violence. For example, 60 percent of women who have been sexually assaulted...have been attacked more than once" (note 16, 157). It is on the basis of these kinds of determinations that Laura Brown, a forensic and clinical psychologist, has argued that "to admit that these everyday assaults on integrity and personal safety are sources of psychic trauma, to acknowledge the absence of safety in the daily lives of women and other nondominant groups, admits what is deeply wrong in many sacred institutions and challenges the benign mask behind which everyday oppression operates" (1995: 105).

Dominic's *The Queen of Peace Room* details numerous instances of such everyday oppression and contributes to our understanding of its complex legacies. As evidence of a broader grammar of gendered violence, it may be tempting to read Dominic's story as "emblematic"—that is, as standing for or symbolic of all the stories of, in this case, violence against women in the second half of twentieth-century North America. However, an ethic of encounter cautions us to recognize that to foreclose our reading here is to miss something more, something crucial about being addressed to read as a witness (Rosenberg and Simon 2000). What is asked of us is that we stay open to the surprise of a phrase, the image that ruptures through a social numbness, an unexpected detail, an acute observation. "Memories of unspeakable experiences stick to the body like sweat on a hot day" (48). Without this attention, we risk missing the specificities of *her* story, as she tells it here, and, concomitantly, the significance for Dominic of what we are being told. "Fears choking me like a scarf" (70). As Dori Laub, writing in the context of witnessing testimony, reminds us, "testimonies are not monologues; they cannot take place in solitude. The witnesses are talking to *somebody*: to somebody they have been waiting for for a long time" (1992: 70-71). While the first witnesses, in this sense, are the nuns at the retreat with whom Dominic begins to witness and return to herself, as readers of this published text we too are being addressed as "somebody." "I made the decision to move from the isolated grey house so fast there were skid marks on the sky" (72). This is the kind of listening-reading relation that has the potential to bring us, as readers, with our own complex and multifaceted histories of suffering and love, into an encounter with the impacts of traumatic experience—not only for those who have suffered, but also, and crucially, for how such experience brings us to the limits of settled knowledge (Caruth 1995, 1996). "A Rolex ticking on bone" (106).

When we "listen to" *The Queen of Peace Room* on these terms, we hear particular ways in which traumatic events structure and affect sense of self, memory, representation, experience, and time. As Cathy Caruth explains:

> most descriptions [of trauma] generally agree that there is a response, sometimes delayed, to an overwhelming event or events, which takes the form of repeated, intrusive hallucinations, dreams, thoughts or behaviours stemming from the event, along with a numbing that may have begun during or after the experience…the event is not assimilated or experienced fully at the time, but only belatedly, in its repeated *possession* of the one who experiences it. (1995, 4)

Dominic's narrative begins in an "isolated retreat house" (9) where she has gone, on the occasion of her fiftieth birthday, to face and come to terms with the violence that had been a part of her life. While the text, then, begins with knowledge of violence as a structuring force of her life, this knowledge comes belatedly; it is not assimilated in the moment of the experiences of abuse, rape, and battering.

Dominic tells us this in a range of ways. She gives testimony, for example, to the sexual abuse by her maternal grandfather—the one she can name only as "the other grandfather" (17)—an indication of the immense risk and wretchedness of this telling that she needs to write in a red pen, "like a cinder that's been smoldering for almost half a century" (18). Smoldering, because this experience has been largely engulfed in silence and in an effort *not to look*. In her descriptions of the sexual abuse by her grandfather, she is at pains to tell us that there was little talk and, when there was, it was directed at her silence. She writes: "I was told to be quiet. Not to tell anyone about anything" (18), while her grandfather's glass eye sits on the dashboard staring, but unseeing. She continues: "In this solitude of spruce and birch and maple, this grandfather would remove my clothing and put his hands inside me, silently looking straight ahead, except for the eyeball sitting on the dashboard. I looked straight ahead too, through the dirty car window, up to the sky" (18).

Trying not to look, not to speak, and, by implication then not to know (for how could one know this and continue as usual?), she writes:

> I tried to get away from the little girl sitting on the
> front seat of that car, looking through the dusty win-
> dow. I tried to get away…I tried to get away…I tried to
> get away from her all my life, but it was useless.…I
> tried to get away from it, to run from it in my mind, but
> her eyes would stare back at me for the rest of my life.
> And the eyes were haunting and unrelenting. (19-20)

In the lexicon of traumatic experience, what Dominic is articulating here are strategies of "dissociation," efforts to separate one's self from the experiences that cannot be integrated, that break the frames of understanding. Judith Lewis Herman explains that one expression of dissociation in abused children is a state of "frozen watchfulness" (1992, 100 citing Ounsted, 1972)—a state that certainly seems consistent with

Dominic's descriptions. What we see in Dominic's text are tactile examples of the possession that Caruth gestured to above; recall for example the stare of her younger child self: "her eyes would stare back at me for the rest of my life…haunting and unrelenting." In addition, she makes reference to the nightmares that began around the time of the abuse and intrusive thoughts/prayers during the day that she would be in a car accident and die (19).

We might also note here her descriptions of passing out, being diagnosed with epilepsy, and her sense of living as two versions of herself. As she explains, following the child abuse testimony, "just as a machine knows when it's overloaded, so does the brain. Abuse and silent images were mounting and blurring and the body finds a coping mechanism. It shuts down…I passed out cold, on the kitchen floor, like one of those winter rabbits" (27). She continues, "I'd been getting dizzy and falling for years, but no one ever talked about it. As if there were two of me, the one who fell and the one who didn't" (27). This articulation is strikingly similar to how trauma researchers Bessel A. Van Der Kolk and Onno Van Der Hart describe living after a traumatic event. They explain: "many traumatized persons…experience long periods of time in which they live, as it were, in two different worlds: the realm of the trauma and the realm of their current day life" (1995: 176). It is this "separation" of selves, brought about, I suggest, not only by the experiences themselves, but also by the not-seeing, not-talking, not-knowing that surrounds Dominic, which make it possible, for example, for a doctor and later a police officer (in relation to the rape in New York) to wonder if she is "a nervous person" (27) or has "a nervous disorder" (38). Such diagnoses treat a person as if she were separate from, or discontinuous with what has been done to her. They risk an individualizing and psychologizing explanation that misses what is crucial: Dominic's "nervousness" (fainting, dizziness) are not inherently about her as a person but manifest *as a response* to unbearable experiences of suffering. For, as Laura Brown reminds us, "personality develops in a complex web of interaction between the internal, phenomenological experiences of the individual and the external, social context in which that person lives" (1995: 103, citing Lermer).

But the book we hold in our hands does not simply document acts of suffering one after the other. Rather, what has as much presence and significance here are the diverse and daily ways in which Dominic survived. These range from a reliance on trees, sky, and earth as an abiding presence when no person was listening—"through all of this the sky stayed with me. Never once leaving. Never once having anywhere else to go. Whenever I woke up, it would be there" (40)—to the community of nuns with whom Dominic finds listening, gentleness, and importantly, recognition. She writes, "a group of nuns in the woods have noticed me. And are responding" (75). Deceptively simple, this statement is enormously important in the context of the narrative, for, to recall Laub again, these nuns are her first (human) witnesses. Between these ends of a continuum, Dominic tells us of a series of other expressions of her agency—her capacity to survive, to resist, to act on her own behalf, to articulate a sense of will—in and through conditions of constraint and threat. I am thinking, for example, of the ways she uses language as a site of naming, and thus, an articulation of *her* reality, as she has lived it. A vivid example here, for me, is toward the end of her remembering her grandfather's abuse; she writes: "[a] calmness didn't exist on the trees near the car where my grandfather sat. Where I sat next to him." Then: "NO! He was sitting next to me. I was NEVER sitting next to him" (20, original emphases). Moving next to project her agony in those times onto the trees "doubled over in pain" (20), Dominic's NO! is a no she couldn't articulate in that car in Newfoundland, but in speaking it now, belatedly, it works as both an injunction (never again!) and a reminder that she is not to blame, she didn't stay in that car by choice. As an adult, facing the threat of attack in New York City, she tells us of fumbling to get her keys, running upstairs to her apartment, screaming on the street when she sees the man a second time. While none of these acts was enough to protect her from the assault, they remind us that to read Dominic as a "passive victim" is to miss how she endeavoured to resist the violence directed at her.

Against the regimes of silencing, perhaps Dominic's most apparent expression of resistance and agency is this self-representation, *The Queen of Peace Room*. As a writer, poet, artist, and curator, Dominic brings to bear on her experiences, her life, creative skills, and knowledge that shape the creation of this as a literary work, with a particular structure and form that's attentive to the workings of time and memory. Organized through a sequence of eight days at the retreat, Dominic's text covers a short span of time in the present, while simultaneously travelling through close to fifty years of (her) history. Contrary to prevailing notions of time as linear, in which "the past" is understood as entirely distinct from and prior to "the present," time, for Dominic, has a far less rigid structure. Like Margaret Atwood's narrator in *Cat's Eye*, "You don't look back along time but down through it, like water. Sometimes this comes to the surface, sometimes that, sometimes nothing. Nothing goes away" (3). Dominic deploys contrasting narrative techniques to bring different aspects of her past to the surface of the present, disrupting a linear sense of both time and narrative. In the case of non-traumatic memories, she uses a writerly style (one that is quite consistent with everyday experiences of memory), in which an image in the present recalls an image in the past, that image becoming impetus for another layer of her story.

Our first encounter of this strategy in the text is on page 5, as she writes of entering the "large brick building" of the retreat house for the first time. Walking through the chapel, she writes: "I don't remember the first time I went to church. I know its name." Her next paragraph begins: "Saint Henry's. A low-ceilinged chapel beneath an elementary school." From this sentence we get our first detailed introduction to her life as a child in the 1940s and '50s. Here we learn something of the church she attended, of her parents, of being schooled by nuns, of the Chinese restaurant fire in town, and of the broader social and political realm into which she was born—toward the end of World War II with early glimpses of the atrocity of the "Final Solution," a generation, she tells us, "weighed down with the past" (6). Dominic's text moves seamlessly from this story of her past forward again into the present at the retreat house with this sentence: "it was [my father's] unshakeable belief…that led me on a search for churches in every city I ever lived in, ever spent more than a weekend in for the rest of my life" (8). And then, "we're shown the kitchen area" (8). As readers, we know we are in the writer's now—however fleetingly, for, after just a paragraph, the radio in that kitchen "flashes" her to another radio in the 1950s and her layered story continues.

While elements of these past experiences might be fraught and disconcerting, they are not "traumatic"—in the sense of numbed to or disassociated from in the moment, only to be "experienced" belatedly. We can see this through a contrast in textual strategies: whereas Dominic's self-representation moves between past and present largely propelled by an image or a reference in the now, sometimes, the past-present shift is more abrupt, as if a piece of the story breaks through the present-day narrative, rather than being recalled by it. In this case, at the level of the writing itself, we are alerted to the distinct unassimilable character of Dominic's experiences of childhood abuse and adult rape. The clearest example is the section marked-off from the rest of the text by the divider on pages 19 (opening) and 20 (closing). The section begins and ends in the meadow at the retreat house, that space and place where Dominic is finding healing and peace, "now." It is in that meadow at midnight—as she is being seen by the "eyes of night" (30)—that Dominic remembers and gives testimony to her experience in New York City in the 1960s of being assaulted, raped at knife-point, and stalked by a man unknown to her. Vividly detailed, the account includes her suicide attempt and her family's reinforcement of silence—both hers and theirs (41). It is noteworthy that the section is closed off here with the divider, an indicator, I am positing, of the need to keep this memory separate—looked at and seen, but too raw to assimilate. As she notes shortly after, "we're required to look back. Not to stay there. But to look back" (45). I speculate that to let this memory bleed textually into others is to risk, precisely, "staying there," with what is, perhaps, still only minimally bearable. While the divider is a fragile guard against this bleeding, it nonetheless works as a signifier, marking a distinction between past and present, the surviving self and the self that holds the traumatic memory.

It is noteworthy that Dominic can do the work of looking back only from a safe present. What makes her present safe enough is the retreat, which, she reminds us repeatedly, is "remote" and where her bedroom is in a building accessed only through a "secret code." Given the ways in which time works in the text, "remote" becomes an intriguing signifier: for, on one level, the retreat is remote from New York City and Newfoundland, from further risk, from people who have harmed her. By literally removing herself from her home, remote here signifies a sense of separateness and calm. Paradoxically, it is this physical remoteness in the present that provides a condition for allowing the past to become proximal, now not remote at all in time, but infusing the present. What makes it possible for Dominic to face that past, she tells us, are the meadow, the nuns, a sense of spirituality, a return to religion, and, I suggest, the significance of the building as secure. Over and over again, Dominic mentions entering the secret code to enter that building. This is not an irrelevant detail, but stands in marked contrast to the car where her grandfather abused her, the vulnerability of walking the streets, an unlocked apartment building door—those spaces and sites where she could not protect herself, could not rely on a physical boundary to keep out those who would violate her.

Towards the end of her eight days at the retreat, Dominic has a dream in which she no longer is afraid, in which the people of her life neatly line the road, divided into those, on one side, who have "caused her pain" and those on the other, who have "brought happiness" (76). This is a healing dream, an expression of her having come to terms with, encountered, and faced the past that has haunted her for most of her lifetime, leaving her now with a sense of "harmony." In the epilogue, Dominic continues, "the future is far. The past is gone. There is only this present, to cherish" (99). We are left with a knowledge that Dominic's journey and writing through suffering, pain, and anguish have led her to a place of peace, an openness to the present, and a renewed sense of possibility. As witness-readers, what we are left with is the responsibility to carry what we have learned from *The Queen of Peace Room* into our families, our neighbourhoods, our cities—not simply to repeat what we know of Dominic's life, but to take up that knowledge as an urgent call against what we have learned to tolerate as normal.

Works Cited

Atwood, Margaret. 1988. *Cat's Eye*. Toronto: McClelland and Stewart.

Britzman, Deborah P. 1998. *Lost Subjects, Contested Objects*. Albany: SUNY Press, 1998.

Brown, Laura. 1995. "Not Outside the Range: One Feminist Perspective on Psychic Trauma." In *Trauma: Explorations in Memory*, edited by Cathy Caruth, 100-72. Baltimore: Johns Hopkins University Press.

Caruth, Cathy. 1996. *Trauma: Explorations in Memory*. Baltimore: Johns Hopkins University Press.

Duffy, Ann, and Rina Cohen. 2001. "Violence against Women: The Struggle Persists." In *Feminist Issues: Race, Class and Sexuality*. 3rd ed., edited by Nancy Mandell, 134-66. Toronto: Prentice-Hall.

Felman, Shoshana, and Dori Laub. 1992. *Testimony: Crises of Witnessing in Literature, Psychoanalysis and History*. New York: Basic Books.

Gilmore, Leigh. 2001. *The Limits of Autobiography: Trauma and Testimony*. Ithaca: Cornell University Press.

Herman, Judith Lewis. 1992. *Trauma and Recovery: The Aftermath of Violence—From Domestic Abuse to Political Terror.* New York: Basic Books.

Marcus, Sharon. 1992. "Fighting Bodies, Fighting Words: A Theory and Politics of Rape Prevention." In *Feminists Theorize the Political,* edited by Judith Butler and Joan W. Scott, 385-403. London and New York: Routledge.

Rosenberg, Sharon and Roger I. Simon. 2000. "Beyond the Logic of Emblemization: Remembering and Learning from the Montréal Massacre." *Educational Theory* 50 (2): 133-55.

Simon, Roger I., Sharon Rosenberg, and Claudia Eppert, eds. 2000. *Between Hope and Despair: Pedagogy and the Remembrance of Historical Trauma.* Lanham, MD: Rowman and Littlefield.

Van Der Kolk, Bessel, and Onno Van Der Hart. 1995. "The Intrusive Past: The Flexibility of Memory and the Engraving of Trauma." In *Trauma: Explorations in Memory,* edited by Cathy Caruth, 158-82. Maryland: Johns Hopkins University Press.

Selected Texts of Related Interest
(Canadian Emphasis)

Allison, Dorothy. 1995. *Two or Three Things I Know for Sure*. New York: Dutton.

Danica, Elly. 1988. *Don't: A Woman's Word*. Charlottetown, PEI: Gynergy Books (available through Canadian Scholars' Press and Women's Press, Toronto).

Danica, Elly. 1996. *Beyond Don't: Dreaming Past the Dark*. Charlottetown, PEI: Gynergy Books (available through Canadian Scholars' Press and Women's Press, Toronto).

Fraser, Sylvia. 1997. *My Father's House: A Memoir of Incest and Healing*. Toronto: Doubleday Books.

Lewis, Tanya. 1999. *Living Beside: Performing Normal after Incest Memories Return*. Toronto: McGilligan Books.

Gahlinger, Claudia. 1993. *Woman in the Rock*. Charlottetown, PEI: Gynergy Books.

MacDonald, Ann-Marie. 1997. *Fall on Your Knees*. Toronto: Vintage.

Warland, Betsy. 1993. *The Bat Had Blue Eyes*. Toronto: Women's Press.

Williamson, Janice. 1994. "Writing Aversion: The Proliferation of Contemporary Canadian Women's Child Sexual Abuse Narratives." In *By, For and About: Feminist Cultural Politics*, edited by Wendy Waring, 197-233. Toronto: Women's Press.